ECOLOGICAL CRISIS

Oliver BARRETT

ECOLOGICAL CRISIS
In Catholic Social Teaching

Domuni-Press

2023

THIS BOOK IS PUBLISHED
BY DOMUNI-PRESS
RESEARCH COLLECTION

Theology & Society

ISBN: 978-2-36648-202-7
© DOMUNI-PRESS, April 2023

www.domuni.eu

I would like to dedicate this book to my late Grandmother Nellie McShane who instilled in me a deep appreciation and love for the Catholic faith.

"Earth's crammed with heaven,
and every common bush afire with God,
But only he who sees takes off his shoes;
the rest sit round it and pluck blackberries"

Elizabeth Barrett Browning (1806-1861)

Abstract

This book begins with an in-depth examination of the issues causing the climate emergency, it's based on the premise that the root cause of the ecological crisis is a moral crisis within humanity. I study in depth both the Old and the New Testament, to discover the Judeo-Christian theology of creation and the proper place of humanity within this framework. I document the development of Catholic Social Teaching in relation to the *cosmos*, examining the publications and contributions from Pope John Paul II, Pope Benedict XVI and Pope Francis. I study in-depth the main themes running through *Laudato Si'* as this is the first time catholic social teaching related to the environment is elevated to the level of an encyclical. I examine how the teaching within *Laudato Si'* will challenge modern lifestyles and worldviews. I advocate the re-establishment of the link between creation and the liturgy and the rediscovery the Trinitarian dimension of creation spirituality.

In the second part of this book, I examine the origins and impact of three popular models of creation, the dominion, the stewardship, and the kinship-community model of creation. I examine the connection between the teaching of Jesus in Matthew 6: 25-33 and the community model of creation as taught by St. Francis of Assisi, the patron of Ecologists. I examine the opportunity the climate emergency presents for ecumenism through the study of teaching from other churches, particularly the Greek Orthodox Church, and joint statements from the Catholic and Greek Orthodox Church.

Keywords: Solidarity, Ecological Conversion. Integral Ecology, Human Ecology, Technocratic Paradigm, Kinship – Community Model of Creation,

Introduction

The first cases of COVID-19 were reported on the 31st of December 2019 when WHO's Country Office, in the Peoples Republic of China, picked up a medical statement by the Wuhan Municipal Health Commission on cases of 'viral pneumonia'. The statement was published on the Wuhan's Municipal Health Commissions' website. The Country Office notified the International Health Regulations focal point in the Who Western Pacific Regional Office and provided a translation of it. In less than a month, on the 20th-21st January 2020, WHO conducted its first mission to Wuhan and met with public health officials to learn about the response to the cluster of cases of the viral pneumonia known as 'novel coronavirus'. By the January 30th, WHO Director- General Dr Thedros Adhanom Ghebreyesus declared the COVID-19 outbreak to be a public health emergency of international concern[1]. It was the scenario the public health community had feared where a dangerous virus emerges and spreads rapidly around the world. In less than one year there have been over 94 million confirmed cases of COVID-19 and the global pandemic has claimed the lives of over two million people[2].

More research is needed to understand the link between the global pandemic and the ecological crisis although scholars are already beginning to make a connection. For example, on the 8th of April 2020 Austin Ivereigh asked Pope Francis, in an interview for 'The Tablet, if he saw the crisis as a chance for ecological conversion, for reasserting priorities and lifestyles? Pope Francis responded with

---

[1] World Health Organization, *A year without precedent: WHO's COVID-19 response,* [website], 2020, A year without precedent: WHO's COVID-19 response, (accessed 20th January 2021).

[2] WHO Coronavirus Disease (COVID-19) Dashboard, [website], 2021, WHO Coronavirus Disease (COVID-19) Dashboard | WHO Coronavirus Disease (COVID-19) Dashboard, (accessed 20th January 2021).

a Spanish saying that 'God always forgives, we forgive sometimes, but nature never forgives'. He is making the point that recent events are nature's response to our current levels of production and consumption[3]. Although more research is required to discover the root cause of the COVID-19 pandemic, the ecological crisis is providing us with an opportunity to take the decisive step from misusing nature to reconnecting with and contemplating nature. Pope Francis makes this point in his recent encyclical, *Fratelli Tutti,* when he states that this health crisis is giving us an opportunity to re-access the way in which we live our lives. Our worst response to the pandemic would be to "… plunge even more deeply into feverish consumerism and egotistical self-preservation"[4].

The ecological crisis is multidimensional. In this project I will focus on the proper place of humanity within God's creation. It is evident we are no longer living in harmony with nature as is evidenced by climate change and the catastrophic impacts on human and natural systems[5]. This is due in part to the process of industrialisation and attempts to mechanise nature. A utilitarian worldview is causing modern man to plunder the earth's resources to meet our own immediate needs. Such action is justified with the claim of infinite resources, growth, and development. We know of course this is not true as our rates of extraction is placing ecosystems at tipping point. The challenge will be to urgently change the mentality of dominion over nature to alliance with nature before we do irreparable damage.

Pope Francis refers to the unbridled consumerism and consumption of the twenty first century as the 'technological

---

[3] Austen Invereigh, *Pope Francis says pandemic can be a 'place of conversion'*, [website], 2020, Pope Francis says pandemic can be a 'place of conversion' (thetablet.co.uk), (accessed 20th January 2020).

[4] Pope Francis, Fratelli Tutti: On Fraternity and Social Friendship, [website], 2020, Fratelli tutti (3 October 2020) | Francis (vatican.va), (accessed 26th January 2020).

[5] The Core Writing Team Synthesis Report IPCC (ed), Rajendra K. Pachauri Chairman IPCC, Leo Meyer Head, Technical Support Unit IPCC, *Climate Change 2014 Synthesis Report*, [Web Site], 2014, (accessed 24th September 2020) https://www.ipcc.ch/site/assets/uploads/2018/02/SYR_AR5_FINAL_full.pdf.

paradigm'[6]. This concept is referred to as 'technocracy and describes mankind seeking mastery over nature through technological advances. Richard Bauckham writes, "The whole of the modern scientific-technological project of dominating nature and exploiting its resources for the good of humanity presumed that total mastery of the Earth's natural processes was within human grasp"[7]. It is doubtful if humankind will ever have total mastery of nature for a variety of reasons. Advocates of technocracy claim there is a technological solution to the climate crisis. Technological advances are important and move us forward however they often create ethical and moral dilemmas. A variant of this ideology, referred to as "therapeutic technocracy" has emerged in America in recent years. It promises that by listening to both science and the voices of the suffering, the nation's physical and psychological health may be ensured[8]. This ideology unites therapeutic belief in empathy, compassion, and concern with faith in technocratic expertise to justify the elite technocrats right to rule. It is built on the premise that technology will sooth the nations pain however it presents difficulties in gauging its success due to its ability to promise more and deliver less. This ideology has plunged humanity into a deep spiritual crisis as we continue to pillage the earth resources. This is creating issues related to equality and social justice as developed nations take advantage over weaker developing nations. Today we are treating the environment as a self-service restaurant and not as a gift with self-transcendent possibilities through the enduring action of the Holy Spirit[9].

Our exploitation of the Earth's eco-systems, fuelled by market-driven capitalism, is causing a loss of biodiversity and is a cause of concern for both present and future generations. This presents a challenge for ecologists and theologians alike as two separate crises

---

[6] Pope Francis, *Laudato Si': On Care for Our Common Home*, London, Catholic Truth Society, 2015, p.55.

[7] Richard Bauckham, *Bible and Ecology*, London, Darton Longman and Todd, 2019, p.4.

[8] Matthew Schmitz, 'Joe Biden's real creed', Catholic Herald, Advent 2020, p.48.

[9] Dermot A. Lane, *Theology and Ecology in Dialogue*, Dublin, Messenger Publications, 2000, p.7.

emerge one environmental and the other social (*LS* 139)[10]. The myth of infinite growth needs to be urgently replaced with an integral ecology brought about through ecological conversion. This will only be achievable when we broaden our concept of salvation and redemption to include the *cosmos* as well as humanity.

---

[10] Pope Francis, *Laudato Si': On Care for Our Common Home*, London, Catholic Truth Society, 2015, p. 69.

The Ecological Crisis

What exactly is the ecological crisis? There is an abundance of scientific evidence to confirm we are in the middle of a climate emergency. This is apparent, for example, when we examine the levels of carbon dioxide in the earth's atmosphere. In the 1990's we passed the sustainable limit of 350 parts per million in the atmosphere[11]. In February 2020, global atmospheric carbon dioxide reached 413ppm[12]. This is the highest level of carbon dioxide in the earth's atmosphere in over 800,000 years. Although there is a natural greenhouse effect, human activity, such as burning fossil fuels for energy, is contributing to the green-house effect in a unique way. The result is human-induced global warming and a negative effect on our climate. Global warming is causing the earth's oceans to increase in temperature, making them more acidic and making it more difficult for marine life to extract calcium from the water to build shells and skeletons. The increase in the temperatures of the oceans is causing Ice Caps to melt and sea levels to increase. High temperatures are having a negative effect on the pollinators in the grain belts threatening the earth's breadbaskets. The crisis is teaching us of the need to rediscover and appreciate a correct relationship with the environment in everyday life[13]. The main ecological issues have emerged and been identified only in last half a century. This is mainly because most of the damage to the environment has been done in the last two hundred years. For this reason, most Catholic Social teaching

---

[11] M. Lorbiecki, *Following St. Francis: John Paul II's Call for Ecological Action,* New York, Rizzoli ex libris, 2014, p. 41.

[12] U.S. National Oceanic and Atmospheric Administration, *Climate Change: Atmospheric Carbon Dioxide*, [website], 2020, https://climate.gov/news-features/understanding-climate/climate-change-atmospheric-carbon-dioxide, (accessed 15th October 2020).

[13] Pope Benedict XVI, *The Garden of God: Toward a Human Ecology,* Washington D.C., The Catholic University of America Press, 2014, p. 33.

related to the environmental issues has been published post Vatican II. Previous teaching related to the dignity of humanity without any particular focus on the interconnectedness of humanity and the environment.

In this research project we will examine the ecological issues in the light of teaching from Saint John Paul II, Pope Benedict XVI and Pope Francis. Saint John Paul II has contributed the most to the climate debate due to the length of his pontificate. His thought provides the building blocks for the most recent contribution from Pope Francis' with the publication of his encyclical *Laudato Si'*[14]. As the urgency to address ecological issues emerged so did the response and guidance from mother church. Previous teaching related to environmental issues seemed to be escapist, binary, and dualistic. For example, an update to the Roman Missal after the council of Trent (1545-1563) states "Lord teach us to despise the things of the earth and to love the things of heaven". The purpose of this project is to understand how creation theology may assist us in our response to the climate emergency. First let us examine the main ecological issues.

---

[14] Kevin W. Irwin, *A Commentary on Laudato Si': Examination the background, Contributions, Implementation, and Future of Pope Francis's Encyclical*, New York, Paulist Press, 2016, p. 14-15.

Ecological Issues

The Green House Effect

The first issue leading to the climate crisis is known as the 'Green House Effect'. Human activity, our excessive use of fossil fuels, has accelerated global warming and caused the loss of biodiversity in many regions. Heavy-duty extraction processes increase substantially the number of Green House gases emitted. Even natural gas extraction can cause leaks in carbon dioxide and methane into the earth's atmosphere. The resulting depletion of the ozone layer and related green-house effect has reached crisis proportions. This is a consequence of industrial growth, massive urban concentrations, and increased demand for energy. In 1990, in a message on the World Day of Peace, Pope John Paul II writes... "Industrial waste, the burning of fossil fuels, unrestricted deforestation, the use of certain types of herbicides, coolants, and propellants: all of these are known to harm the atmosphere and the environment. The resulting meteorological and atmospheric changes range from damage to health, to the future submersion of low-lying lands"[15]. As early as 1990, Pope John Paul, refers to the degradation of the environment as a 'crisis' indicating the extremity of the situation at that time. The IPCC special report on global warming states we have to aim for 1.5°C global warming to achieve sustainable development goals. This will require systematic change and assist in the fight against poverty and the restoration of parity between developing and developed countries.

According to the IPCC report all countries need to raise their level of ambition and enhance institutional capabilities to utilize

---

[15] Pope John Paul II, *Peace with God the Creator, Peace with all of Creation*, [Website], 1990, http://www.vatican.va/content/john-paul-ii/en/messages/peace/documents/hf_jp-ii_mes_19891208_xxiii-world-day-for-peace.html, (accessed 17th October, 2010).

indigenous and local knowledge. What the report is effectively saying is that the answer to a first world problem can be found by following the example and lifestyle of indigenous people in the third world. Interestingly this point is also made by Pope Francis, in *Querida Amazonía,* when he compares the actions of multinational companies who "cut the veins of our mother earth"[16] to those of the original peoples of the Amazon region whose wisdom inspires care and respect for creation with a clear consciousness of its limits.

One certain way to reduce global warming is through fossil fuel diversification and finding alternative sources of energy e.g., solar energy, wind energy, and electric storage technologies. There is also the option for nuclear energy and carbon dioxide capture and storage in the electricity sector, however the nuclear option to avoid greenhouse gases has raised important moral questions. This is firstly because of the burning of fossil fuels in the mining and processing of uranium and secondly because water sources are depleted and polluted by cooling and storage of nuclear rods and cores.[17] There is also the possibility of a nuclear disaster and the cataclysmic destructive power of nuclear weapons. Pope John Paul II deeply questioned the threats the nuclear option posed to humanity. These threats include terrorism, natural disaster and the moral question of the transportation and long-term storage of waste. The disposal of harmful nuclear waste on the land of indigenous peoples is referred to as 'environmental racism'. Acts of 'environmental racism' are an example of the moral character of the ecological crisis and indicate any attempt at fossil fuel diversification will only be effective and sustainable when considered morally acceptable. This means the alternatives will not have a negative effect on the eco-system and weaker nations.

There is the moral obligation for countries to be responsible and take action to offset carbon emissions and become carbon neutral. The Vatican, for example, the smallest country in the world, is leading the way in this field and has recently begun to cultivate a several- hundred-acre climatic forest in Bükk (Hungary) thus

---

[16] Pope Francis, *Querida Amazonia*, Hampshire, Redemptorist Publication, 2020, p.26.

[17] M. Lorbiecki, *Following St. Francis: John Paul II's Call for Ecological Action,* New York, Rizzoli ex libris, 2014, p. 113.

becoming the first climatically neutral country[18]. Costa Rica, New Zealand, Norway, Iceland, and the Maldives are also renewing their economies and social structures to become carbon neutral.

Although there is no explicit mention of fossil fuel diversification in the Scriptures, St. Paul speaks of the need for the liberation of the non-human material world (*ktsis*) from futility and the bondage of sin (Romans 8: 19-23). John Bolt refers to Romans 8: 19-23 as an 'environmental mantra'[19]. According to the book of Genesis, the chaotic state and frustration of the non-human material world is due to the sin of Adam (Gen 3: 15-17). However, God's covenant relationship is both with humanity and the non-human material world as both strive towards the same cosmic goal. We read this in Genesis chapter nine when Yahweh's promise to Noah is made "between myself and you and every living creature" (Gen 9: 12-13). The covenant is made with all of creation including the natural world.

Deforestation

Plants and trees are the natural technology the Earth uses to absorb carbon dioxide. They are an integral part of the eco-systems and necessary to offset carbon emissions. They are a vital source of oxygen. Human activity, such as deforestation, is affecting the natural process of growth and regrowth and accelerating unnatural desertification causing drought in the places like the Americas. The tree is important for biodiversification and is an important symbol of life within the Judeo-Christian faith. Marybeth Lorbieckei describes he tree as "...a living metaphor and ecological canary in the mineshaft"[20].

Deforestation is not a modern phenomenon and is referenced by scholars in antiquity. Two non-Christian historians, Josephus and

---

[18] Pope Benedict XVI, *The Garden of God: Toward a Human Ecology*, Washington, The Catholic University of America Press, 2014, p. 9.

[19] John Bolt, *The Relation between Creation and Redemption in Romans 8: 18-27*, Michigan, CTJ, 1995, cited in Richard Bauckham, *Bible and Ecology: Rediscovering the Community of Creation*, London, Darton Longman and Todd, 2019, p. 100.

[20] M. Lorbiecki, *Following St. Francis: John Paul II's Call for Ecological Action*, New York, Rizzoli ex libris, 2014, p. 131.

Aelius Aristides, use the Greek word *gymnos,* meaning to make naked, to describe Rome's stripping of forests. Josephus laments at the deforestation of the countryside around Jerusalem by the Romans[21]. He makes a direct connection between deforestation, warfare, and the disturbance of peace. When this takes place, it represents one nations domination over another nation as is the case with the Romans and the Jewish people. The same Greek word, *gymnos,* is used in an eschatological context in the book of Revelation to refer to the second action against Babylon (Rev. 17:16). There are ecological implications when a landscape stripped of vegetation and forest[22].

Pope John Paul II recognised the importance of reforestation as early as 1987. In his homily on the Feast of St. John Gualbert he stated the conservation and the development of forest heritage, in any area, is essential for the maintenance and re-composition of the natural balances' indispensable to life. For the pontiff, reforestation will play an important role in reversing much of the damage we have done to the environment in the last four hundred years[23]. It restores sustainability and a natural balance to the ecosystem converting toxic carbon dioxide into life giving oxygen. One of the main reasons for the urgency is deforestation and forest degradation is affecting vulnerable populations living in the earth's tropical rainforests in Africa, Asia, South and Central America. Deforestation occurs in these regions for economic reasons e.g., to pay foreign debts. Tropical deforestation, as in the Amazon region, is the direct result of local and international economic interests. The impact of deforestation has far reaching social consequences impacting the economy and the environment at a local and global level.

The pace at which deforestation is occurring is alarming. The European Commission reported in 2017 that one football pitch of

---

[21] Barbara R. Rossing, *River of Life in God's New Jerusalem: An eschatological Vision for the Earth's Future,* in Dieter T. Hessel and Rosemary Radford Ruether, *Christianity and Ecology,* Cambridge Massachusetts, Harvard University Press, 2000. p 211.

[22] Ibid.

[23] Pope John Paul II, *Homily on the Occasion of the Feast of St. John Gualbert,* [website], 1987, http://www.vatican.va/content/john-paul-ii/it/homilies/1987/documents/hf_jp-ii_hom_19870712_messa-val-visdende.html, (accessed 18th October, 2020).

forest was lost every second and 13 million hectares of tropical rainforest, approximately the size of Greece, are lost every year[24]. This is significant considering it is estimated the tropical rainforests house 170,000 of the earth's 250,000 known plant species, provide important economic resources, and containing extracts for over 121 prescription drugs[25]. The biodiversity of the tropical rainforests not only contributes to maintaining the ecological equilibrium of the planet's eco-system, but it is also essential to indigenous communities who depend on the biodiversity for their health, nourishment, and preservation of culture. Colonizing interests of the timber and mining industries are expelling and marginalizing indigenous peoples, forcing migration to the outskirts of cities where their human dignity is threatened through enslavement, subjection, and poverty[26]. The actions of economic actors are ignoring the rights and the dignity of the original peoples of the Amazon causing deforestation to be an ecological justice issue.

The injustice and lack of respect for the dignity of the indigenous Amazonian people was condemned by Pope Benedict XVI in 2007. Speaking to the youth in São Paulo he stated… "The devastation of the environment in the Amazon Basin and the threats against the human dignity of peoples living within that region call for greater commitment in the different areas of activity than society tends to recognise."[27]. If anything, the Amazon rainforest has taught us of the importance of preserving the culture of the indigenous population and the need to collaborate with the original peoples to sustain the ecosystems of the tropical rainforests. This sentiment is echoed by Dr Maathai, foundress of the Green Belt Movement in Kenya. The Green Belt movement is a successful tree planting

---

[24] European Commission Deforestation and forest degradation, [website], https://ec. europa.eu/environment/forests/deforestation.htm, (accessed 18th October 2020).

[25] M. Lorbiecki, *Following St. Francis: John Paul II's Call for Ecological Action*, New York, Rizzoli ex libris, 2014, p. 133.

[26] Pope Francis, *Querida Amazonia*, Hampshire, Redemptorist Publication, 2020, p.10.

[27] Pope Benedict XVI, *Apostolic Journey of his Holiness Benedict XVI to Brazil on the occasion of the fifth General Conference of the Bishops of Latin America and the Caribbean: Meeting with Youth*, [website], 2007, http://www.vatican.va/content/benedict-xvi/en/speeches/2007/may/documents/hf_ben-xvi_spe_20070510_youth-brazil.html, (accessed 18th October, 2020).

movement established by Dr Maathai to offer work to the poor women in the foothills of Mount Kenya. Dr Maathai recognised that economic marginalisation and impoverishment in Africa is partly because the decisions effecting the economic and political life of the original population are being taken by the ruling elite. The policies and decision of the ruling elite are facilitating the siphoning of the wealth of indigenous communities, literally from under their feet. In the process they are marginalised and disempowered economically, denied access to information, knowledge, and resources, and forced to over mine their environment, thereby jeopardizing even their future generations[28].

The exclusion of indigenous people from the decisions directly affecting their future is criticised by religious leaders around the globe. Pope Francis in *Querida Amazonía* states that original peoples have the right to thorough and straightforward information about projects which may affect them, so they may give or withhold consent to these projects and can propose acceptable alternatives[29]. He goes on to say that there is a need to establish a legal framework to ensure the protection of ecosystems from the technological paradigm otherwise they may overwhelm politics, freedom, and justice[30]. The pontiff listens acutely to both the cry of the earth and the cry of the poor. He suggests that the rights of original peoples and their indigenous ways of life within vulnerable ecosystems such as the Amazon, should be preserved and enshrined in law to protect them from the exploitation of stronger nations.

The forest, *maquis,* features often within the Hebrew tradition and is a wilderness, a place of chaos and danger. The book of Isaiah reminds us the wilderness can only become a fruitful field through the work of the Holy Spirit (Isa. 32:15). In Genesis God brings order to the chaos and creates an orchard-forest called 'Eden' (Gen 2: 8-15). The trees in the garden are beautiful and produce edible fruit (Gen 2:9). We know from the book of Ezekiel that Eden was a well-

---

[28] Dr Maathai, *Bottlenecks to Development in Africa*, [website], 1995, http://greenbelt movement.org/wangari-maathai/key-speeches-and-articles/bottleknecks-to-development-in-africa, (accessed 18th October, 2020).

[29] Pope Francis, *Querida Amazonia,* Hampshire, Redemptorist Publication, 2020, p.30.

[30] Ibid., p.31.

watered place of divine blessing (Ezek 31: 8-9). In the Song of Songs, the exotic garden of sweet-scented plants is compared to a bride (Cant. 4: 12-15). This image captures the life-giving properties of the garden created for humanity (Gen 2: 15). The book of Genesis reminds us of God's presence in the garden (Genesis 3:8). Joshtrom Isaac Kureethadam states the sin of modern man, as with the first man Adam, is the denial of God's presence in the garden therefore regarding humanity and the world as autonomous[31]. However, it is essential for human identity to establish a proper relationship with creation. It is only in recognising and contemplating the transcendent source of creation we accept our responsibility as stewards[32]. According to the New Testament our salvation, necessary for the disregard we have shown to divine limitations (Gen 2: 16-17), is inextricably linked with the cross of *Jesus Christ*.

Oceans and Marine Life

Human activity, as with the Mauritian Oil Spill in July 2020, is having a negative effect on our oceans[33]. In the last decade there are an ever-increasing number of examples of ocean distress as human activity is changing the chemistry of the Oceans and depleting crucial ocean species. Increased ocean temperatures, due the absorption of excess carbon, is causing the ice at the Earth's poles to melt e.g., in Montana's Glacier National Park the number of Glaciers has declined to fewer than thirty from more than 150 in 1910[34]. The effects of global warming that would naturally occur in geological time are now happening in a human lifetime. The melting ice is causing the sea levels to rise each year and wildlife in the polar regions are being affected by the rising sea temperatures. The rise in atmospheric and ocean temperatures is increasing the frequency and intensity of

---

[31] Joshtrom Isaac Kureethadam, *The Ten Green Commandments of Laudato Si*, Minnesota, Liturgical Press, 1994, p. 79.

[32] Pope Benedict XVI, *The Garden of God: Toward a Human Ecology*, Washington D.C., The Catholic University of America Press, 2014, p.64.

[33] BBC News, *Mauritius oil spill: Fears vessel may 'break in two' as cracks appear*, [website], 2020, https://www.bbc.co.uk/news/world-africa-53722701, (accessed 24th Oct 2020).

[34] Daniel Glick, *The Big Thaw*, [website], (accessed 24th October 2020), https://www.nationalgeographic.com/environment/global-warming/big-thaw/.

hurricanes and storms even creating super storm phenomena such as Typhoon Haiyan. As Glaciers store approximately three quarters of the earth's fresh water there will be less available, and it is estimated droughts will become more common with parts of the US facing 'megadroughts' by 2100[35].

The ocean is a vital source of food for billions of people, and it is estimated each person consumes 35 pounds of sea food each year. High-tech and often pervasive illegal fishing practices is causing overharvesting of the ocean species with certain species such as Bluefin Tuna and Grand Banks Cod being caught faster than their reproduction rate[36]. Overharvesting is having a negative effect on food security. Pope John Paul II, in an address to the Fishermen of Newfoundland in 1984, encouraged small fishing operations over the operations of multinationals and oligarchies. He is critical of large intensive fishing operations and how they affect the financial independence of small family fishing operations and the way they compromise the common destination of goods. His message is founded on *Jesus'* commandment to love and to server each other. Opening and closing his address with *Jesus* calling the disciples from their fishing boats on the Sea of Galilee, he asks for careful stewardship of the Oceans for the sea to continue to offer its harvest. This may only be achieved through international collaboration and long-range planning to ensure the equal distribution of the Earth's resources[37].

Another factor compromising the harvest from the sea is the increased number of pollutants, particularly single use plastics, which are being dumped into the oceans. The tonnes of plastic entering the oceans each year is resulting in entanglement and ingestion by marine life. This is having a negative effect on human health through exposure to chemicals through the food chain and is costing the

---

[35] National Geographic, *Effects of Global Warming,* [website] (accessed 24th October 2020), https://www.nationalgeographic.com/environment/global-warming/global-warming-effects/.

[36] World Wildlife, *Overfishing,* [website], What is Overfishing? Facts, Effects and Overfishing Solutions (worldwildlife.org), (accessed 24th October 2020).

[37] Pope John Paul II, *Address of Pope John Paul II To Members of the Fishing Community,* [website], 1984, (accessed 24th October 2020) http://www.vatican.va/content/john-paul-ii/en/speeches/1984/september/documents/hf_jp-ii_spe_19840912_pescatori-terranova.html.

tourism and the fisheries sector millions of Euros each year[38]. Chemical and nuclear waste is polluting our oceans and finding its way into the food chain as many of the toxins go into the marine species and end up in the cells in our bodies. Over development in coastal regions is destroying the natural shoreline and displacing tidal communities

The Oceans, especially in the Judeo-Christian tradition, have a primary place in creation. Genesis 1: 1-3 begins with the earth being formless. The Hebrew word used here, *tōhû*, occurs twenty times in the entire Old Testament and means without shape or form indicating in the beginning the Earth is entirely uninhabitable by human beings[39]. In verses two to five of Genesis chapter one, God forms and names what is formless with his spirit moving over the waters. The message in the text is God is master over all of creation (Psalm 104: 6 -7). God both creates an ordered cosmos from disorder and controls the forces opposed to that order including the uncontrollable ocean force (Job 38: 8-11). The rebelliousness of the Oceans is personified in Leviathan, a chaos monster. (Job 41, Psalm 74, 104). The name is transferred mythologically to the Devil as both the sea and Leviathan represent the destructive forces in the world threating the divine order. Ancient Israel had a deep sense of the destructive power of the raging ocean. God's act of creation placed the waters of chaos within strict limits, ordering them and it is God who continues to control the Chaos. There is an eschatological dimension to the chaos as only at the end of time will the chaos finally be abolished (Isa. 27:1)[40]. Our disregard for the divine limitation placed on life giving resources of the earth, including the Oceans, is causing chaos and disorder. This creates an urgent need to establish the proto-logical harmony described in the book of Genesis[41].

---

[38] *Plastic in the Ocean: the facts, effects and new EU rules,* [website], 2018, https://www.europarl.europa.eu/news/en/headlines/society/20181005STO15110/plastic-in-the-ocean-the-facts-effects-and-new-eu-rules, (accessed 24th October 2020).

[39] Richard J. Clifford, S.J. and Roland E. Murphy, O. Carm. *Genesis,* in Raymond E. Brown, Joseph A. Fitzmyer, Roland E. Murphy (ed.), *The New Jerome Biblical Commentary,* London, Geoffrey Chapman, 1990, p. 10.

[40] Richard Bauckham, *Bible and Ecology,* London, Darton Longman and Todd, 2019, p.60-61.

[41] Pope Benedict XVI, *The Garden of God: Toward a Human Ecology,* Washington D.C., The Catholic University of America Press, 2014, p.64.

Water Supply and Purity

One percent of the earth's water is usable by humans and it is not evenly distributed. The Middle East is an example of one geographical regions effected by the supply of water. There is the possibility of water wars in our near future with military strategists predicting that ongoing tensions regarding the uneven distribution of shared water supplies will lead to conflict. For example, access to water supplies is one of the reasons for the Israeli-Palestinian conflict[42]. There are chronic water shortages not only in the Near East but also in Africa, northern Asia, and Australia. This is due to supply and pollution caused by man who is not respecting the goods of the earth and polluting formally clean waters. One of the reasons for the problem of water supply is that corporate rights are taking precedence over the rights of individual citizens. As businesses and investors seek to create a profit from the privatization of public water supplies many Christians are questioning the morality of such actions as this will guarantee drinkable water only for the affluent, those who can afford it.

Millions of people lack access to safe water and billions urgently need improved sanitization[43]. Many people are forced to walk long distances every day to fetch drinkable water from unreliable water sources. Clean water is a fundamental human right and making it available to all represents a huge development challenge. In his Lenten message in 1993 Pope John Paul II urged people of good will to seek solutions to desertification, pollution, and privatization of water…

> Furthermore, it is quite clear to everyone that uncontrolled industrial development and the use of technologies that disrupt the balance of nature have caused serious damage to the environment and caused grave disasters. We are running the risk of leaving as our heritage to future generations the

---

[42] Agnese Carlini, *The Major Role of Water on the Israeli-Palestinian Conflict*, [website], 2015, https://guides.library.uwa.edu.au/ld.php?content_id=14872881, (accessed 27th October 2020).

[43] The Water Crisis, [website], https://water.org/our-impact/water-crisis/, (accessed 27th October 2020).

tragedy of thirst and desertification in many parts of the world[44].

There are definite ethical questions surrounding the privatization of water by multi-national corporations and many social implications for the poor in societies. As companies buy up the springs and clean water sources then water becomes solely for the affluent. This is a contentious issue, not only in developing, also in developed countries as in Italy in 2011 a law was passed to privatize water supply. This sparked outrage and a public referendum ensued. In 2012 the Constitutional Court determined the decree law as unconstitutional and cancelled it[45]. Catholic social teaching is adamantly against the privatization of water as it is contrary to the concept of the common destination of goods, and it creates issues related to social and ecological justice. *Gaudium et Spes* states clearly that God intended the Earth with everything contained in it for the use of all human beings. For this reason, attention must always be paid to the universal destination of earthly goods and man should regard the things he legitimately possesses in the common sense to benefit others[46]. When we read *Gaudium et Spes* we are compelled to question the legitimacy of claims to private ownership of the earth's resources. The privatization of water will have a knock-on effect for the environment due to the pollution from the making of single use plastic[47].

Pollution from Industry is directly making its way into our rivers and oceans as occurred in 1986 when a fire at Basel chemical plant caused tonnes of toxic pesticides to leak into the river Rhine[48].

---

[44] Pope John Paul II, *Message of his Holiness Pope John Paull II for Lent in 1993,* [website], 1993, http://www.vatican.va/content/john-paul-ii/en/messages/lent/documents/hf_jp-ii_mes_1909 1992_lent-1993.html, (accessed 27th October 2020).

[45] European Water Movement, *Summary of the Re-municipalization of the Water Service in Italia,* [website], 2020, http://europeanwater.org/actions/country-city-focus/323-summary-of-the-remunicipalization-of-the-water-service-in-italia, (accessed 31st October 2020).

[46] Pope Paul VI, *Gaudium et Spes,* [website], 1965, (accessed 31st October 2021) http://www.vatican.va/archive/hist_councils/ii_vatican_council/documents/vat-ii_cons_ 19651207_gaudium-et-spes_en.html.

[47] M. Lorbiecki, *Following St. Francis: John Paul II's Call for Ecological Action,* New York, Rizzoli ex libris, 2014, p. 165.

[48] Imogen Foulkes, *Rhine on path to recovery,* [website], 2001, http://news.bbc.co.uk/ 1/hi/world/europe/1371142.stm, (accessed 31st October 2020).

From the 1950s to the 1970s the Rhine was referred to as the sewer of Europe as waste from industry, agriculture and shipping gradually polluted this important waterway over time making it difficult for sensitive salmon stocks to replenish and survive along with flora and fauna. Two years after the chemical spillage Pope John Paul II visited the Rhine to highlight the importance of restoring its ecosystem. The Rhine represents what can be achieved when an action plan is put in place and countries collaborate to create cleaner water and allow biological repair of a natural ecosystem. In 2020 it is reported the water quality has improved significantly with almost all of households and industries connected to purification installations, a reduction in nutrient and metal discharge points and an increase in plant and animal species[49]. The Rhine represents an example of our ability to restore a damaged ecosystem.

According to the Psalms, water is essential for life. It is God who makes the spring gush fourth to quench the thirst of his creatures and irrigate the soil. God waters the mountains and the trees of the Lebanon (Psalm 104: 10-13, 16). God is the source of the life-giving waters of the Earth (Genesis 2: 8-15). It is the Lord who responds to the thirst of his people with actions, creating flowing rivers atop mountains and desert valleys (Isaiah 41: 17-19). The prophet Ezekiel describes the water as flowing from the Temple as he envisions the new Temple (Ezekiel 47: 1, 9-12). Ezekiel's new Temple description is eschatological as it is not concluded in the book of Revelation. In his vision a river of freshwater flows from the Temple, through the Kidron valley to the Dead Sea. Although the language is mythical, in the Old Testament Scriptures, water is a God given gift and symbolises fertility and life-giving power[50]. Water is the source of life for trees, living creatures and a source of food.

The eschatological visions in the book of Revelation have added significance when we interpret them ecologically. The author John contrasts the 'New Jerusalem', a place of ecological justice,

---

[49] International Commission for the Protection of the Rhine, *The New story of the Rhine our lifeline*, [website], 2020, https://ourrhine.eu/, (accessed 31st October 2020).

[50] Lawrence Boadt, C.S.P., *Ezekiel*, in Raymond E. Brown, Joseph A. Fitzmyer, Roland E. Murphy (ed.), *The New Jerome Biblical Commentary*, London, Geoffrey Chapman, 1990, p. 327.

with the violence, injustice, and ecological imperialism of Babylon. The fountain of living water is the central image in the 'New Jerusalem' (Rev. 21:6, 22; 22:17; Rev 7:17) where God establishes a gift economy (*dōrean*). According to Barbara A. Rossing, the author of Revelation alludes to Isaiah's invitation to everyone who thirsts to come to the water[51]. This is in direct contrast to the exploitative economy of Babylon. The living waters of the 'New Jerusalem' in the book of Revelation speak for the real waters of our world. The 'New Jerusalem's' promise of access to pure, living water for all offers a prophetic critique of our damage to eco-systems, of waters polluted by industrial and agricultural waste and encroachment of wetlands by developers. At a time when the waters of life on our planet are in danger of dying the vision of the river of life can sustain our commitment to justice and healing for all creation[52].

Chemical and Industrial Pollution

The Chernobyl nuclear disaster in April 1986 is one example of an ecological disaster caused by humanities ability to wreak havoc on the environment. It is estimated the eighteen-mile radius around the contaminated area, referred to as the exclusion zone, will not be habitable for at least twenty thousand years[53]. Pope Paul VI in 1971 referred to the pollution of the material environment as a permanent menace causing wide-ranging social problems concerning the entire human family[54]. The issue of pollution becomes even more critical when the pollution is nuclear as the effects of nuclear waste are having a devastating effect on humanity and ecosystems. Pope John Paul II made a direct connection between disrespect for nature and the threat to world peace. Speaking to the children of Chernobyl fifteen years after the disaster he stated "Recalling the tragic effects

---

[51] Barbara R. Rossing, *River of Life in God's New Jerusalem: An eschatological Vision for the Earth's Future*, in Dieter T. Hessel and Rosemary Radford Ruether, *Christianity and Ecology*, Cambridge Massachusetts, Harvard University Press, 2000. p 216.

[52] Ibid.

[53] Erin Blakemore, *The Chernobyl disaster: what happened and the long-term impact*, [website], 2019, https://www.nationalgeographic.co.uk/environment/2019/05/chernobyl-disaster-what-happened-and-long-term-impact, (accessed 1st November, 2020).

[54] Pope Benedict XVI, *The Garden of God: Toward a Human Ecology*, Washington D.C., The Catholic University of America Press, 2014, p. 40.

caused by the accident of the nuclear reactor in Chernobyl, let us think of the future generations that these children represent. We must prepare a future of peace, free of fear and similar threats. This task is for everyone[55]". International collaboration is essential to ensure a nuclear disaster, like Chernobyl, does not happen again. Pope John Paull II confirms this when he advocates an internationally coordinated approach to the management of the earth's resources. He writes… "In many cases the effects of ecological problems transcend the boarders of individual states; hence their solution cannot be found solely on a national level"[56].

We need to consider responsibility and accountability for ecological disasters. Although Thomas Jefferson warned in 1816 about the dangers of making corporations into immortal persons in the eyes of the law, corporations now have personhood status making it difficult to hold decision makers accountable[57]. The destruction of the environment is often a consequence of decisions made by private interests. This raises ethical questions as the selfish quest for good fortune displays no regard for the expectations of future generations. An example of this is the process of globalization causing agriculture to be intensified and increasing the use of harmful chemicals. The indiscriminate use of advances in science and technology may have devastating long term effects[58]. We must realize when we interfere with natural cycles in the environment are not preserving creations integrity and diverge from God's plan.

Nuclear incidents have a far-reaching effect and have health implications for populations far from the place where the incident occurs. This is one of the reasons for the need for international

---

[55] Pope John Paul II, Address of John Paul II to the Children of Chernobyl and their Hosts, [website], 2001, http://www.vatican.va/content/john-paul-ii/en/speeches/2001/april/documents/hf_jp-ii_spe_20010426_chernobyl.html, (accessed 1st November, 2020).

[56] Pope John Paul II, *Message of his Holiness Pope John Paul II for the Celebration of the World Day of Peace* , [website], 1990, http://www.vatican.va/content/john-paul-ii/en/messages/peace/documents/hf_jp-ii_mes_19891208_xxiii-world-day-for-peace.html, (accessed 07/11/2020).

[57] M. Lorbiecki, *Following St. Francis: John Paul II's Call for Ecological Action,* New York, Rizzoli ex libris, 2014, p. 280.

[58] Pope John Paul II, *Ecclesia in America,* [website], 1999, http://www.vatican.va/content/john-paul-ii/en/apost_exhortations/documents/hf_jp-ii_exh_22011999_ecclesia-in-america.html, (accessed 07/11/2020).

collaboration from different disciplines to find alternatives to nuclear energy and to prevent nuclear incidents from occurring. Often the sources of chemical pollution are close to those communities who are less affluent causing 'environmental racism' to occur. These communities are found in what is termed 'Developing Countries' and their inhabitants are less protected due to the absence of environmental regulation. Often children, for example, grow up next to substandard lead-acid battery recycling plants increasing the levels of lead in their blood[59]. The obvious double standards of environmental regulation between developing and developed countries is immoral and unethical. Pope John Paul II rightly identified the chemical hazards in developing countries are often imported from more affluent countries who profit from the legislative weakness of poorer countries. He writes… "It would be difficult to overstate the weight of the moral duty incumbent on developed countries to assist developing countries in their efforts to solve their chemical pollution and health hazard problems"[60]. Each nation has the responsibility to the moderated use of the earth's resources and to work together to safeguard the environment for future generations.

The various types of pollution air, water, ground, noise are undoubtedly due to the intervention of man in the macro environment of nature[61]. Modern ecology and science studies the effects between human activity and its consequences for the well-being of the non-human world. The Old Testament prophets were acutely aware of this long before the advent of modern technology. In the Old Testament we find many examples of non- human praise of creation and lament of the human desecration of God's creation through pollution and degradation. The prophet Jeremiah makes a direct connection between the disharmony in creation and the disorientation of

---

[59] Clarios Foundation, *Pure Earth, Clarios Foundation and UNICEF launch Protecting Every Childs Potential: A Future Free from Lead Exposure*, [website], 2020, https://www.prnewswire.com/news-releases/pure-earth-clarios-foundation-and-unicef-launch-protecting-every-childs-potential-a-future-free-from-lead-exposure-301151687.html, (accessed 07/11/2020).

[60] Pope John Paul II, *Address of his Holiness Pope John Paul II to the Participants in the Workshop on "Chemical Hazards in Developing Countries" organised by the Pontifical Academy of Sciences*, [website], 1993, http://www.vatican.va/content/john-paul-ii/en/speeches/1993/october/documents/hf_jp-ii_spe_19931022_rischi-chimici.html, (accessed 07/1/2020).

[61] Paul Haffner, *Mystery of Creation*, Herefordshire, Gracewing, 2010, p.286.

humanity from God's plan. He writes... "Even the stork in the heavens knows the times; and the turtledove, swallow and crane observe the time of their coming; but my people do not know the ordinance of the LORD" (Jeremiah 8:7). Jeremiah compares the way in which the non-human world observes cycles and their orientation toward the creator compared with the ignorance of humanity to the 'big picture'. Violence toward the environment, when placed in a moral framework, is sinful[62]. This gives rise the relatively modern phenomena of ecological sin.

War and Conflict

War has a devastating effect on the environment and on the lives of people living in conflict zones. One example of this is the dropping of two atomic bombs on the Japanese city of Hiroshima and Nagasaki during August of 1945 killing more than 140,000 people. Shusaku Endo gives the following account of the events...

> The plutonium-239 bomb exploded in Nagasaki with the equivalent force of twenty-two thousand tonnes of conventional explosives but with vast differences. Setting aside for the moment the A-bomb's lethal radiation, there was the intense heat, which reached several million degrees centigrade at the explosion point. The whole mass of the huge bomb was ionized, and a fireball created, making the air around it luminous, emitting ultraviolet rays and infrared rays and blistering roof tiles farther than a half a mile from the epicentre.[63]

Although the dropping of the A-bombs signified the end of the Second World War, it caused the beginning of the Cold War. The loss of human life continued afterwards as tens of thousands died later of radiation exposure[64]. Everything within a mile radius of the drop zone was killed and the environment totally devastated. The fall

---

[62] Guy P. Couturier, C.S.C., *Jeremiah*, in Raymond E. Brown, Joseph A. Fitzmyer, Roland E. Murphy (ed.), *The New Jerome Biblical Commentary*, London, Geoffrey Chapman, 1990, p. 327.

[63] Shusaku Endo, *A Song for Nagasaki*, San Francisco, Ignatius press, 1988, p. 157.

[64] *Bombing of Hiroshima and Nagasaki*, [website], 2009, https://www.history.com/topics/world-war-ii/bombing-of-hiroshima-and-nagasaki, (accessed 8th November 2020).

out resulted in contamination of, not only the surrounding area, but caused radioactive particles to travel for hundreds of miles[65]. Writing to scholars participating in a study week on 'Resource and Population' in 1991, Pope John Paul II identified war as the worst cause of environmental damage[66]. Although countries, due to scientific and technological advancements, have changed the way they wage war, the only way to prevent war is through dialogue, meditation, and sanctions[67].

Our definition and concept of war has changed in recent decades. The Cold War, for example, conditioned Americans to view security threats as those posed by hostile nations and not to consider the threat to human life posed by climate change. One lesson we may take from the current pandemic is how central ecological security is to national global security concerns[68]. The decision by President Joe Biden in January of 2021 to re-join the Paris Climate accord and to keep the US in the World Health Organisation represents an important milestone in the recognition of the global biosphere as a foundational and a vast superpower to be respected. Another aspect of the biosphere as a superpower is evident when we consider natures retaliatory capacity against human ecological irresponsibility[69]. With the increased occurrence of extreme types of weather, we have realized nature's sometimes devastating power over humanity.

The environmental effects of a small-scale war, as with the Gulf War for example, are often long term e.g., Kuwait's aquifer remained contaminated for years. Not only is there an environmental

---

[65] Kylie Lemon, *Environmental Effects of the Atomic Bomb,* [medium], 2018, https://scien cing.com/environmental-effects-atomic-bomb-8203814.html, (accessed 8th November 2020).

[66] Pope John Paul II, *Address of his Holiness Pope John Paul II to Scholars Participating in the Study Week on Resource and Population,* [website], 1991, http://www.vatican.va/ content/john-paul-ii/en/speeches/1991/november/documents/hf_jp-ii_spe_19911122_risorse-popolazione.html, (accessed 8th November, 2020).

[67] Pope John Paul II, *The Fifth General Assembly of the United Nations organisations: Address of his Holiness John Paul II,* [website], 1995, http://www.vatican.va/content/john-paul-ii/en/speeches/1995/october/documents/hf_jp-ii_spe_05101995_address-to-uno.html, (accessed 8th November 2020).

[68] William C. French, 'Ecological Security and Policies of Restraint' in Dieter D. Hessel (ed) and Rosemary Radford Ruether (ed), Chri*stianity and Ecology,* Massachusetts, Harvard University Press, 2000, p.486.

[69] Ibid.

cost to warfare there is also a human cost causing the death of civilians, soldiers and population displacement creating refugees. Advancements in science and technology have increased the means for countries to wage war. As these are often inhumane this creates new moral and ethical dilemmas e.g., Pope Francis condemned the inhumanity of the use of chemical warfare in Syria in 2013[70]. Environmental devastation is not only the result of war it is often the cause of war. Pope John Paul II, celebrating the World Day of Peace in 1990, identified lack of respect for nature and the plundering of natural resources as a threat to world peace. He writes…

> Today, any form of war on a global scale would lead to incalculable ecological damage. But even local or regional wars, however limited, not only destroy human life and social structures, but also damage the land, ruining crops and vegetation as well as poisoning the soil and water. The survivors of war are forced to begin life in very different environmental conditions, which in turn create situations of extreme social unrest, with further negative consequences for the environment[71].

Warfare often results in irreversible ecological damage as the destruction of natural resources, resulting in a sharp decline in the quality of life, can send societies over the cliff like lemmings to war[72]. This is concept has been proven throughout history. The prophet Jeremiah provides a description of land devastated by war when both Gilead and Lebanon were two regions known for their forests (Jer 22:6-7). The Jewish author Josephus provides us with a non-scriptural reference. He uses the term *erēmoō* to describe the destruction of the landscape by the Roman armies. In ancient antiquity scholars made the connection between respect for the environment and longstanding peace between nations.

---

[70] Pope Francis, *Angelus*, [website], 2013, http://www.vatican.va/content/francesco/en/angelus/2013/documents/papa-francesco_angelus_20130901.html, (accessed 8th November 2020).

[71] Pope John Paul II, *Message of His Holiness Pope John Paul II For the Celebration of the World Day of Peace*, [website], 1990, http://www.vatican.va/content/john-paul-ii/en/messages/peace/documents/hf_jp-ii_mes_19891208_xxiii-world-day-for-peace.html, (accessed 08th November 2020).

[72] M. Lorbiecki, *Following St. Francis: John Paul II's Call for Ecological Action*, New York, Rizzoli ex libris, 2014, p. 298.

Poverty

The process of globalization is accelerated by technology and the material progress it brings. Technology has its obvious advantages in the way it allows people to connect regardless of their location. Pope Francis, in *Laudato Si'*, acknowledges the way in which technology has remedied many of the countless evils which limit and harm human beings. He expresses gratitude at the technological advancements in the fields of medicine, engineering and communication that have contributed to making development sustainable[73]. Issues arise when advancements in technology are not accompanied with an equal advancement of human responsibility. When we use technical advancements irresponsibly this may cause the relationship between humans and material things to be confrontational e.g., when we extract more of the earth's resources than necessary under the false pre-tense there is a limitless supply. This is the false pre-tense upon which the 'technocratic paradigm' is founded, and it leads only to the misuse of power and dominance over the Earth and weaker nations. It leads also to the impoverishment of weaker nations as profit becomes a motivating factor in decision making without regard for the economically marginalised.

Leading age technology is increasing production however this in turn is dispensing with human labour. This is perverse as the prevailing system of accumulation accompanied by consumer lifestyles is responsible for the technology that is gradually replacing the workforce. Technological progress is often ecologically inappropriate, burdening eco-systems and creating unsustainable forms of development. We question if this technology may be considered as progress as it is obviously inhumane to place commodities and the market at the centre. Pope Benedict XVI reminds us that man cannot be dominated by technology or subjected to it[74]. He states there is an imperative need to prioritise the development of human ecology and we should not approach nature

---

[73] Pope Francis, *Angelus,* [website], 2013, http://www.vatican.va/content/francesco/en/angelus/2013/documents/papa-francesco_angelus_20130901.html, (accessed 8th November 2020).

[74] Pope Benedict XVI, *The Garden of God: Toward a Human Ecology,* Washington D.C., The Catholic University of America Press, 2014, p. 73.

as a place of exploitation and play[75]. When technology manipulates and controls human and non-human life the resulting attitude is harmful to the integrity of humanity and the non-human world. Another criticism of technology is that it is not socially integrated i.e., it does not produce benefits for all societies but only for those countries controlling scientific and technical production[76]. Too often we seek technical fixes to environmental and social problems to avoid making the necessary changes to social structures and institutions.

Often it is vulnerable and developing countries that are exploited for their natural resources to produce goods for multinational companies in developed countries. Donal Dorr states that even the use of the term 'developing countries', to describe what were really poor countries only serves to ease the consciences of those who are well off in the face of abject poverty of millions of people. He goes on to state that even the term 'development' is not true development rather a type of exploitation[77]. Donal Dorr is making the point that our definition of under-development is a construct of those nations exploiting the resources of other countries. There is a need to redefine our concepts as only development which is sustainable is to be considered authentic development. Dermot A. Lane is cautious regarding the interpretation of the term 'sustainable development'. He states the new rhetoric of 'sustainable development' needs to be scrutinised carefully. He states that this popular slogan is often a coded way to maintain the status quo, and the concept is highly ambiguous, conceptually vague, and open to manipulation[78]. This sentiment is express by Pope Francis in his Apostolic Exhortation *Querida Amazonia* when he states...

> In this regard, we can take one step further and note that integral ecology cannot be content simply with fine-tuning

---

[75] Pope Benedict XVI, *The Garden of God: Toward a Human Ecology,* Washington D.C., The Catholic University of America Press, 2014, p. 73.

[76] Leonardo Boff, *Cry of the Earth, Cry of the Poor,* New York Maryknoll Press, 1987, p. 65.

[77] Donal Dorr, *Option for the Poor: A Hundred Years of Vatican Social Teaching,* Dublin, Gill and Macmillian, 1983, p.181.

[78] Dermot A. Lane, *Theology and Ecology in Dialogue: The Wisdom of Laudato Si',* Dublin, Messenger Publications, 2020, p.19.

technical questions or political, juridical, and social decisions. The best ecology always has an educational dimension that can encourage the development of new habits in individuals and groups...A sound sustainable ecology, one capable of bringing about change, will not develop unless people are changed, unless they are encouraged to opt for another style of life, one less greedy and more serene, respectful, less anxious, more fraternal[79].

We must address the imbalance in the access to and consumption of the earth's goods. Leonardo Boff refers to our planet as 'spaceship Earth' with one fifth of the population in the passenger section and the other four-fifths are in the cargo hold. The population in the passenger section consume eighty percent of the supplies for the journey whereas the other four-fifths suffer cold, hunger and all kinds of hardship[80]. What Leonardo Boff is referring to here is the disparity among nations in terms of consumption of the earth's resources and the resulting ecological injustice. The social consciousness of communities in so called developing countries is gradually being heightened as these nations are gradually becoming aware of the reasons for the imbalance. One common reason is there is the unjust and unequal distribution of the Earth's goods and services. Another is that many of the poor developing countries were once former colonies. These countries suffer from resource degradation and depletion and are bound to the 'first world' in crippling debt[81]. The ever-increasing gap between the rich and the poor can lead to conflict and compound existing conflicts which in turn further fuels poverty. Pope John Paul II, speaking for the celebration of 'World Day of Peace' stated that proper ecological balance will only be achieved by directly addressing structural forms of poverty that exist throughout the world[82]. Pope John Paul II is referring to here is to structural injustice which is the systemic root

---

[79] Pope Francis, Querida Amazonía, The Amazon: New Paths for the Church and for an Integral Ecology, Hampshire, Redemptorist Publications, 2020, p. 33

[80] Leonardo Boff, Cry of the Earth, Cry of the Poor, New York, Maryknoll Press, 1987, p. 111.

[81] M. Lorbiecki, Following St. Francis: John Paul II's Call for Ecological Action, New York, Rizzoli ex libris, 2014, p. 174.

[82] Pope John Paul II, Peace with God the Creator, Peace with all Creation, [website], 1990, http://www.vatican.va/content/john-paul-ii/en/messages/peace/documents/hf_jp-ii_mes_1989 1208_xxiii-world-day-for-peace.html, (accessed 14th November 2020).

of material poverty. Poverty is also prolonged by the lack of participation of those who are marginalised in determining their own destiny. In 1968 Church leaders from Latin America gathered at Medellín in Colombia to address the issue of structural injustice upholding and fostering dependency and poverty. The documents from the conference refers to injustice as being institutionalised. They refer to poverty as not just something that happens, rather it is caused by human action particularly the situation of internal colonialism and external neo-colonialism[83]. In other words to tackle poverty we need to first address and reorganise the systemic causes of poverty.

As we have mentioned, the current twenty first century model of development, known as the technocratic paradigm, is founded on a myth of unlimited growth[84] . Industrialisation ensures higher rates of production of goods and services every year by drawing more and more resources from the earth. The problem is that this level of production is unsustainable. The United Nation report on 'Our Common Future' (1987), defines sustainable development as a process of change in which the exploitation of resources, the direction of investments, the orientation of technological development, and institutional change are made consistent with future as well as present needs[85]. The report highlights the short sightedness of the current levels of extraction of the earth's resources as a primary risk to sustainable development goals. The process of globalisation necessitates a 'global re-thinking' of the entire problem to reorientate it in a way that is consistent with the fundamental rights of human beings. This is necessary because power, profit and money are being prioritized over the human person and damaging out

---

[83] Donal Dorr, *Option for the Poor: A Hundred Years of Vatican Social Teaching*, Dublin, Gill and Macmillian, 1983, p. 159.

[84] Pope Francis, *Laudato Si*, [website], 2015, http://www.vatican.va/content/francesco/en/ency clicals/documents/papa-francesco_20150524_enciclica-laudato-si.html, (accessed 15th November 2011).

[85] The United Nations, 'Report of the World Commission on Environment and Development', [website], 1987, https://sustainabledevelopment.un.org/content/documents/5987our-common-future.pdf, (accessed 15th November 2020).

integrity[86]. One possible response, advocated by Pope Francis, is referred to as 'God-orientated humanism'. Other possible responses include compassionate capitalism, natural capitalism, and sustainable capitalism. These approaches will cause us to redefine our concept of development. The United Nations utilises a full cost public sector accounting method called 'Triple Bottom Line'. This method tabulates three core elements of people, profit, and planet. Economists have developed national indicators such as Adjusted GDP, the Happy Planet Index, the Index of Sustainable Economic Welfare, and the Eco Budget which measure economic footprint. The aim is to reduce expectations on earnings and growth to be more sustainable. There are now over 840 socially responsible investment funds performing similarly to regular funds e.g., Pax World, Calvert Equity Income Fund and Appleseed Fund[87].

'Social Ecology' refers to the way human beings relate to one another and it is possible to access the relationship between first world countries and third world countries in this context. It is evident from the disparity of lifestyles current economic systems are exploitative and exclusionary. We ought to strive for an economy of what is sufficient for all. Most of the earth's population fall into the excluded category. Human activity over the last hundred years, particularly with the industrial revolutions, has increased this problem. Troeltsch, in the Social Teaching of the Christian Churches (1911), comments…

> The social problem is vast and complicated. It includes the problem of the capitalistic economic period and of the industrial proletariat created by it; and the growth of militaristic and bureaucratic giant states; of the enormous increase of population, which effects colonial and world policy, of the mechanical technique, which produces enormous masses of materials and links up and mobalizes the

---

[86] Pope Francis, *Address of Pope Francis To The Centesimus Annus Pro Pontifice Foundation*, [website], http://www.vatican.va/content/francesco/en/speeches/2013/may/documents/papa-francesco_20130525_centesimus-annus-pro-pontifice.html, (accessed 15th November, 2020).

[87] M. Lorbiecki, *Following St. Francis: John Paul II's Call for Ecological Action,* New York, Rizzoli ex libris, 2014, p. 177-179.

whole world for the purposes of trade, but which also treats men and labour like machines[88].

This is the fundamental error and assumption of the technocratic paradigm, as Troeltsch states, to treat men and the non-human world as a machine thus denying their intrinsic value and place within the natural created order.

Ecological and Climate justice is dependent upon the establishment of social justice through solidarity with the poor. Pope Francis in *Laudatio Si'* reminds us that the ecological crisis has more to do with the plight of the less fortunate brothers and sisters than it has to do with the extinction of polar bears. He says today we must realize that a true ecological approach always becomes a social approach, and we must integrate questions of justice in debates on the environment to hear both the cry of the earth and the cry of the poor[89]. I agree with this point from Pope Francis for when we place the rights of non-human life above the rights of humanity then we descend into Pantheism. It is important here to make the distinction between the worship of the earth itself and the Christian approach to worshipping the Creator of the *cosmos*. The poverty factor highlights the urgent need to prioritize human rights such as the right to life and nourishment, socioeconomic rights and distributive justice, political and cultural rights, and the right to religious liberty[90]. The poor are disproportionate victims of the degradation of our common home[91].

Ensuring the common destination of the earth's resources is one way in which we can restore parity between richer nations and economically weaker nations. The need for solidarity with the poor and marginalised was expressed by Pope Benedict XVI on the visit of Chrysostomos II (June 2007). He appealed to leaders of nations to

---

[88] Ernst Troeltsch, *The Social Teaching of the Christian Churches,* Chicago, University of Chicago Press, 1960, p.1010.

[89] Pope Francis, *Laudato Si,* [website], 2015, http://www.vatican.va/content/francesco/en/encyclicals/documents/papa-francesco_20150524_enciclica-laudato-si.html, (accessed 22nd November 2020).

[90] Leonardo Boff, *When Theology Listens to the Poor*, San Francisco, Harper & Row, 1988, p. 56.

[91] Joshtrom Isaac Kureethadam, *The Ten Green Commandments of Laudato Si',* Minnesota, Liturgical Press, 2015, p.35.

promote the equitable distribution of the earth's goods in a spirit of solidarity with the poor and destitute in the world[92]. In his encyclical *Caritas in Veritate,* he states that for any development to be considered integral it needs to promote the development of every human being[93]. He restated, at an Angelus in Castel Gandolfo (2007), that everyone needs to cooperate to promote the common good, and the development and safeguard of creation. This will serve to strengthen the alliance between man and creation to mirror the creative love of God from whom we come and to whom we are bound[94]. His message is clear, the restoration of ecological justice is dependent upon the establishment of just social structures which make provision to alleviate poverty.

One possible exit strategy for leaving the existing paradigm is to empower those with few resources to be principal builders of a new and human future for everyone. In the *Message of His Holiness Pope John Paul II for the Celebration of the World Day of Peace,* Pope John Paul II makes several important points on this issue[95]. Firstly, within every human being there is a deep need for peace. Secondly, the loss of immense resources is only one of a sequence of horrors which characterised the twentieth century. Thirdly, he states that economic problems do not stem from the lack of resources but from economic, social, and cultural structures which are ill-equipped to meet the demands of genuine development. And fourthly, the poor have a right to share in material goods and be protagonists and agents of their own future development[96]. Our Spiritual leaders emphasise

---

[92] Pope Benedict XVI, *The Garden of God: Toward a Human Ecology,* Washington D.C., The Catholic University of America Press, 2014, p.18.

[93] Pope Benedict XVI, *Caritas In Veritate,* [website], 2009, http://www.vatican.va/content/benedict-xvi/en/encyclicals/documents/hf_ben-xvi_enc_20090629_caritas-in-veritate.html, (accessed 22nd November 2020).

[94] Pope Benedict XVI, *The Garden of God: Toward a Human Ecology,* Washington D.C., The Catholic University of America Press, 2014, p. 104.

[95] Pope John Paul II, *Message of His Holiness Pope John Paul II For the Celebration of the World Day of Peace,* [website], 2000, XXXIII World Day For Peace 2000, "Peace on earth to those whom God loves!" | John Paul II (vatican.va), (accessed 28th November 2020).

[96] Intervention By the Permanent Observer of the Holy See Delegation at the 11th Session of the United Nations Commission on Sustainable Development, [website], 2003, Intervention by H.E. Msgr. Celestino Migliore on Sustainable Development (vatican.va), (accessed 28th November 2020).

time and time again for development to be sustainable we need empower those who are marginalised to be involved in the decision-making process.

The call for sustainable development and the preferential option for the poor are intricately connected. All development efforts need to take into consideration people's ideas and concerns and then share with them the education and technology and funds to create sustainable futures. Sustainable development will be essential for future generations and the long-term global view. God's purposes for creation includes a vision for the future as it is founded upon the covenant relationship which is from generation to generation. The covenant relationship challenges the existing paradigm because it does not fit with the Creator's original design. An important element of sustainable development is the restoration of eco-justice. To achieve this, it is important we address the issues caused by globalization such as the structural perpetuation of poverty. As we have previously stated there is close correlation between economic poverty and ecological poverty as the poor suffer disproportionally from the environmental destruction e.g., plantation farming of commodity crops destroys biodiversity and creates wealth for a few from the labour of the poor. The establishment of sustainable development goals considering the vision of the marginalised will help to deconstruct unjust economic systems which only serve to increase the gap between the rich and the poor.

Oppression of Women

Female oppression is an international phenomenon which is evidenced through inequality in politics, the workplace, and education. In extreme cases it has manifested itself in kidnappings, sex trafficking, sexual violence, the exploitation of women through prostitution and the objectification of women through pornography. What is most disturbing is the normalization of this type of activity in certain societies to give an impression of acceptability. The root cause of this oppression is a dominant attitude towards women to force them into subordination. Pope John Paul II, in his letter to Women in 1995, addressed the central issues. He opened the letter giving thanks to the Holy Trinity for the mystery of women. He outlines the way in which social and cultural conditioning has failed to acknowledge the dignity of women, relegating them to the margins of society and reducing them to servitude. He criticizes the hedonistic commercial culture which exploits women and girls for profit[97]. The hedonistic culture, in modern times, is propagated through social media channels when cyber bulling places undue stress on women to confirm to a certain look or body type. Often due to social conditioning, women are not even aware of their own dignity. I would like to examine the connection between the oppression of women and eco-justice.

It is evident that ecological degradation intersects with the subordination of women and social justice. As this is the case, then one step towards the restoration of eco-justice will be the redefinition of gender relationships within societies. This phenomenon has been identified by eco-feminists who have documented the historical and ideological connections between the subordination of women by men and the exploitation of nature[98]. Any act of violence against men, women and children will have a negative effect on human ecology. Human ecological issues in turn affect society's ability to function and the ability of the people within these societies to work together. Human ecological issues create a culture of waste and contribute to a lack of dignity and respect. An example of a human ecological issue is our failure to recognise women `are an important part of the solution to the ecological crisis[99]. Women unquestionably have a transformative effect on communities, particularly in the field of Ecology. This concept has its roots in the Judeo-Christian faith. In the first pages of the Old Testament Scriptures man finds a partner with whom he can dialogue in complete equality. However, in many parts of the world women face many obstacles to being acknowledged, appreciated, and have their dignity respected. Pope

---

[97] Pope John Paul II, *Letter of Pope John Paul II To Women*, [website], Letter to Women (June 29, 1995) | John Paul II (vatican.va), (accessed 15th January 2021).

[98] Daniel Cowdin, 'The Moral Status of Other Kind in Christian Ethics', in Dieter T. Hessel and Rosemary Radford Ruether, *Christianity and Ecology*, Cambridge Massachusetts, Harvard University Press, 2000. p 278.

[99] Pope John Paul II, *Letter of Pope John Paul II To Women*, [website], Letter to Women (June 29, 1995) | John Paul II (vatican.va), (accessed 15th January 2021).

John Paul II invites women to become teachers of peace and encourages us to reflect on the role of women in family and society and the unique role they play in educating for peace[100].

Many scholars, such as Rosemary Radford Ruether, have made a direct connection between the exploitation of the earth and the subordination of women. Ruether directly connects sexism and ecological exploitation. We see the connection in linguistic metaphors used to describe domination of nature and male hierarchy over women e.g., we talk of the rape of the earth. At the same time in many cultures the earth is referred to as 'Mother Earth' which projects the image of a nurturing and caring mother. Ecological feminism, the study of the interconnection between the domination of women and the domination of nature, represents a challenge to classical Christian theology. I agree there is substantial evidence to suggest there is a definite connection between negative social attitudes towards women and disrespect and exploitation of the environment. The two go hand in hand, where one exists, we find the other. When we believe that members of the human family and animals are our property it can have negative and often violent consequences.

Ecofeminism's criticism of classical theology is that classical theological systems are built upon a theological structure based on a need to dominate, exploit, and conquer. Ecofeminism differs from the hegemonic classical discourse in that it seeks to reinterpret and expand doctrines, such as the Trinity, to include women and the natural world. I believe the value in the eco-feminist discourse is in causing us to rethink our attitude toward women and role of women within vulnerable communities. Ecofeminists such as Ruether and Gebara are proposing a new way of doing theology. They are challenging the existing theological paradigm. By reinforcing the connection between healthy eco-systems and respect for the dignity of women they are ensuring women are an integral part of future sustainable development.

---

[100] Pope John Paul II, *Message of his Holiness Pope John Paul II For the XXVIII World Day of Peace*, [website], 1995, <u>XXVIII World Day for Peace 1995,Women: teachers of peace | John Paul II (vatican.va)</u>, (accessed 13th January 2021).

When we look behind any system of exploitation, we find there are hierarchical dualisms and binary systems. Binary systems are often used to devalue women compared to men[101]. One possible origin for the domination of women and nature is in misinterpretation of the creation story in Genesis. In the Hebrew creation story Eve is formed from Adam (Genesis 2: 21-23). It is the female Eve, seduced by the arrogant angel who used a serpent as a mouthpiece, who tempts Adam to eat the fruit of the tree of knowledge in the Garden of Eden (Genesis 3: 1-7). It is the female Eve who is disobedient to God's limitation and seduces the male Adam to sin causing paradise to be lost. There is no explicit mandate for the subordination of women in the Hebrew creation account, however the female Eve is portrayed as a derivative of the male Adam and responsible for the disharmony in paradise. There is the evidence of cultural subordination of women to men in the Hebrew law e.g., the practice of a levirate marriage is an example of patriarchy. Obviously, it is a mistake to justify the subordination of women because of one passage in Scripture. In fact, Genesis 3:15 is referred to as the 'protoevangelium'... "I will enmity between you and the woman, and between your seed and her seed; he shall bruise your head and you shall bruise his heel". This verse is referred to as the first Gospel because after the fall a figure of a woman emerges as the source of the means of our salvation.

Christianity has often been criticized for perpetuating the patriarchal cosmogony in Hebrew and Greek thought. However Catholic teaching has always challenged the unjust domination of all human beings and encouraged education and equality for women to achieve sustainable development. In Judeo-Christian scriptures the Hebrew word *rua'h,* which describes the spirit of the Lord moving over the earth, is feminine. The book of Isaiah (Isaiah 66:11-14) uses female imagery to explain the motherhood of God and create a sense of peace and contentment. Pope John Paull II, in his apostolic exhortation to Bishops in America in 1999, denounced the domination of the powerful over the weak, discrimination, sexual

---

[101] Dermot A. Lane, *Theology and Ecology in Dialogue: The Wisdom of Laudato Si',* Dublin, Messenger Publications, 2020, p. 35.

abuse, and male domination as contrary to God's plan[102]. The Church upholds the indissolubility of marriage, supports the intellectual development of women, and encourages their vocation to religious orders. Often access to education was only possible by joining religious orders and renouncing the world. Traditionally these orders educated future leaders. The Church reaffirms the need for the biological and intellectual diversity of women for its own ecological and spiritual health to accurately reflect the Creator's original intention for humanity[103].

The ministerial priesthood is an expression of service and not of domination or discrimination. There is an intrinsic need for female involvement in the Church in different fields and at all levels particularly in decision making. What is more their involvement and inclusion in communities challenges models of male domination. Pope Francis more recently acknowledged that the Church cannot be considered complete and whole without the involvement of women and their roles. He stated in an interview in 2013 that broader opportunities for women will make room for their stronger presence in the Church. He said the deep questions asked by women need to be addressed but that he is wary of a kind of female *machismo*. Pope Francis acknowledged women are essential for the church and Mary is of greater importance than the Bishops. We have the responsibility to investigate further the role of women in the church to give them the dignity they deserve. To develop a profound theology of women we must work harder to reflect on their function within the church and decisions should only be made with the involvement of the feminine genius. The challenge today is to think about the specific role of women in those places where the authority of the church is exercised for various areas of the church[104].

The New Testament Scriptures contain numerous examples challenging the cultural norms regarding women in the first century

---

[102] Pope John Paul II, *Ecclesia In America*, [website], 1999, Ecclesia in America (January 22, 1999) | John Paul II (vatican.va), (accessed 16th January 2021).

[103] M. Lorbiecki, *Following St. Francis: John Paul II's Call for Ecological Action*, New York, Rizzoli ex libris, 2014, p. 204.

[104] Antonio Spadaro, S.J., *A Big Heart Open to God*, [website], 2013, A Big Heart Open to God: An interview with Pope Francis | America Magazine, (accessed 16th July 2021).

B.C. *Jesus Christ* is ground-breaking in his attitude toward women (Luke 7: 36-39). Pope John Paul II writes...

> When it comes to setting women free from every kind of exploitation and domination, the Gospel contains an ever-relevant message which goes back to the message of *Jesus Christ* himself. Transcending the established norms of his own culture, Jesus treated women with openness, respect, acceptance, and tenderness. In this way he honoured the dignity which women have always possessed according to God's plan and in his love[105].

One example of this is in the story of the woman caught in adultery in John 7: 53 – 8: 11. The law, as outlined in the book of Deuteronomy (Deut 22: 23-24), prescribed stoning for a married woman who commits adultery. The Romans deprived the Jews the right to carry out the death penalty in cases where their law prescribed it[106]. Jesus does not fall into the trap of rejecting the law of Moses or the authority Rome. Instead, he writes in the ground with his finger and asks whoever is without sin to cast the first stone (Jer. 17:13). Jesus is not ranked among her accusers. She is free to go but not to sin again.

Recourse to the feminine genius will be essential to solving ecological problems. Dr. Amy Caiazza and Allison Barrett, in a 2003 study by the institute for Women's Policy Research, found that women are less likely to support cuts to environmental spending. They are less sympathetic to business when it comes to environmental regulation. Women have more positive feelings towards environmental activists and are particularly concerned about environmental problems that create risks for health and safety especially at local level. Women are more interested in environmentalism to protect themselves, their families, and others. They are less likely to trust environmental institutions to do their job. Although they are less likely to participate politically than men, they

---

[105] Pope John Paul II, *Letter of Pope John Paul II To Women*, [website], 1995, Letter to Women (June 29, 1995) | John Paul II (vatican.va), (accessed 15th January 2021).

[106] Pheme Perkins, 'The Gospel According to John', in in Raymond E. Brown, Joseph A. Fitzmyer, Roland E. Murphy (ed.), *The New Jerome Biblical Commentary*, London, Geoffrey Chapman, 1990, p. 965.

are more likely to volunteer for, and give money to, environmental causes. They are prominent leaders in key areas particularly in environmental movements and in green consumerism[107]. This is evident from those countries who are in a race to become the first sustainable countries in the planet. Costa Rica, New Zealand, Iceland, and Norway are led by women. Germany a country advanced in integrating solar energy, is also led by a women Chancellor Angela Merkel. Women make a positive contribution to social, economic, cultural, artistic, and political life. Women are the first to be hit by environmental issues as they make up 70% of the world's poor. In many indigenous communities, women are gathering firewood, fetching water, cooking, and caring for their families. With investment and training in sustainable development women are well equipped to make the best use of limited resources.

---

[107] M. Lorbiecki, *Following St. Francis: John Paul II's Call for Ecological Action,* New York, Rizzoli ex libris, 2014, p. 196 – 197.

The Ecological Crisis:
A Crisis of Faith and Morality

The ecological issues we have listed are an external symptom of a deeper internal crisis within humanity. This fact is stated by Pope John Paul II, in his message for the celebration of the World Day of Peace in 1990, when he emphasised several times at the root of the ecological crisis is a question of morality. Commentating on the book of Genesis, he explains disharmony is rooted in humanities non-compliance with the Creators plan which manifested itself in the sin of disobedience. Mankind's rebelliousness is accompanied with the earth's rebellion against him (Gen 3: 17-19; 4:12). The central tenet of his message is when we turn back on the Creators plan it leads only to disorder. Pope John Paul II writes...

> People are asking anxiously if it still possible to remedy the damage which has been done. Clearly, an adequate solution cannot not be found merely in better management or more rational use of the earth's resources, as important as these may be. Rather we must go to the source of the problem and face it in its entirety that profound moral crisis of which the destruction of the environment is only one troubling aspect[108].

When we recognise the moral dimension of the ecological crisis then we begin to realise the sinfulness of ecological degradation.

It is possible to identify the main elements of the moral character of the ecological crisis. The first is the indiscriminate application of advances in science and technology. Scientific and

---

[108] Pope John Paul II, *Message of his Holiness pope John Paul II for the Celebration of World Day of Peace: peace with God the Creator, Peace with all of Creation*, [website], 1990, XXIII World Day for Peace 1990,Peace with God the Creator, peace with all of creation | John Paul II (vatican.va), (accessed 29th November 2020).

technological advancements, bringing benefits particularly in the field of agriculture, have caused us to realise interference in the eco-system often has negative consequences. The second is, at the core of the ecological problem there is a disrespect for life itself. Environmental pollution is an example of this disrespect as productivity and economic interests take precedence over the dignity of workers and the good of individuals and entire peoples. Environmental destruction is evidence of a reductionist vision of humanity rooted in contempt for humanity and egotistical self-preservation. Thirdly, biological research and experimentation into the origins of human life itself without consideration to ethical norms could lead to man's self- destruction. Respect for life is the foundation upon which a peaceful society will stand and a lack of respect for nature threatens this peace. We need also to recognise that a harmonious universe is endowed with its own integrity. When we begin to view the environment as integral then we realize the repercussions of our actions towards the natural world. Any action which damages the integrity of the natural world could be considered immoral as it represents a blatant disregard for the future[109].

The source of the ecological crisis, as we previously stated, is the exploitation of most of the earth's resource by a privileged minority. Pope Paul VI, in *Gaudium et Spes,* confirmed God intended the fruits of the earth to be for all humanity[110]. The exploitation of the earth's resources , the result of individual and collective selfishness, is actually contrary to the order of creation[111]. The true state of the natural environment is characterised by biodiversity and mutual interdependence. The interesting point here is the recognition that creation is naturally ordered toward the equal distribution of the earth's resources and it is human activity and the lack of solidarity

---

[109] Pope John Paul II, *Message of his Holiness pope John Paul II for the Celebration of World Day of Peace: peace with God the Creator, Peace with all of Creation*, [website], 1990, XXIII World Day for Peace 1990,Peace with God the Creator, peace with all of creation | John Paul II (vatican.va), (accessed 6th March 2021).

[110] Pope Paul VI, *Gaudium et Spes,* [website], 1965, Pastoral Constitution on the Church in the Modern Word-Gaudium et Spes (vatican.va), (accessed 29th November 2020).

[111] Pope John Paul II, *Message of his Holiness pope John Paul II for the Celebration of World Day of Peace: peace with God the Creator, Peace with all of Creation*, [website], 1990, XXIII World Day for Peace 1990,Peace with God the Creator, peace with all of creation | John Paul II (vatican.va), (accessed 6th March 2021).

that has caused some nations to prosper and others to be impoverished. One possible solution to this issue is internationally coordinated management of the earth's resources, coupled with national monitoring of technological and scientific advances, as a possible solution to the uneven distribution of the earth's resources[112].

The need for solidarity among nations has a moral dimension. For example, developed nations, have a responsibility for restoring the ecological harmony and peace that has been disrupted through their exploitation of the earth's resources. To restore the natural order demands a radical change in lifestyle in the first world from compulsive consumerism to a lifestyle of simplicity, moderation, and discipline. One essential vehicle for this change will be the provision of an education which values ecological responsibility for oneself and others and challenges the existing patterns of thought and behaviour. This is something that will be possible to accomplish through international collaboration. In *Centesimus Annus,* Pope John Paul II refers to man's ability to work in close collaboration with others to transform natural and human environments. He states economic activity cannot only be concerned with supplying enough goods but also should be concerned with the quality of goods produced and consumed. This also applies to the quality of life and environment enjoyed by humanity[113].

Our unbridled desire to accumulate personal wealth is one of the reasons we are not preserving creation for future generations. Our consumerist lifestyle choices are causing us to fail to recognise our deep spiritual dimension of the relationship with creation. We are no longer listening to the cry of the earth and the cry of the poor and instead we are perpetuating the waste of environmental and human resources. One possible remedy to ecological ills will be to re-establish the spiritual dimension of our lives and reconnect with the

---

[112] Pope John Paul II, *Message of his Holiness pope John Paul II for the Celebration of World Day of Peace: peace with God the Creator, Peace with all of Creation*, [website], 1990, XXIII World Day for Peace 1990,Peace with God the Creator, peace with all of creation | John Paul II (vatican.va), (accessed 6th March 2021).

[113] Pope John Paul II, *Centesimus Annus*, 1991, (The Holy See: Papal Archive, 1991), Centesimus Annus (1 May 1991) | John Paul II (vatican.va).

divine source of the gift of creation[114]. This will help us to understand the direct connection between interior and exterior ecology.

Modern man and modern lifestyles have replaced theology with anthropology, and this is another possible source of the ecological crisis. What this means is that humanity is placing itself at the centre of creation and displacing God. We have forgotten that our ability to create and transform our natural environment is based upon God's gift of creation. We have also denied the true purpose of the creation event and tried to become demi-gods. Richard Bauckham states that the theological antidote to the modern mistake is to recognise humans are made in the image of God to exercise dominion on God's behalf, not in God's stead[115]. When man usurps the place of God the result is the twofold. First the destruction of the natural environment and secondly the destruction of the human environment. We then create sinful structures which only perpetuate immoral conditions and diminish the possibility for an authentic human ecology. Often those who are oppressed by these sinful structures do even not realise they are being oppressed. The only way to deconstruct sinful structures within societies is through patience and courage. When we create authentic social structures, founded upon morality, the result is we foster respect for the environment. An authentic human ecology, which cannot simply be safeguarded by market forces, is secured through the guarantee of the common destination of the earth's goods

Numerous other scholars, for example Dermot A. Lane, have also identified anthropocentrism as the central issue at the heart of the modern ecological crisis. Anthropocentrism places humanity at the centre of creation. This grants humanity a licence to dominate the non-human aspects of creation. The issue with anthropocentrism is that it separates humanity from cosmology, the part of metaphysics which deals with the world as a totality of phenomena in time and

---

[114] Pope John Paul II, *Message of John Paul II For the 23rd World Day of Tourism 2002*, (The Holy See: Papal Archive, 2002).

[115] Richard Bauckham, *Bible and Ecology: Rediscovering the Community of Creation*, London, Darton Longman and Todd, 2019, p. 30-31.

space[116]. The process of gradually shifting from theology to anthropology, according to Lane, has been taking place since the late Middle Ages. Anthropology has especially permeated the areas of grace, salvation, and eschatology[117]. Other scholars, such as Charles Taylor, trace the progress of anthropocentrism from belief to unbelief. There are several stages that contributed to the unbelief of humanity starting with the period of Enlightenment, the rise of modernity, and the process of secularization[118]. The last five hundred are marked by the shift from the transcendent to the immanent. We have changed in how we see our humanity. Taylor distinguishes between the open, pre-modern self with a transcendental horizon and the closed, modern self who is disenchanted with the Universe. Dermott A. Lane makes a direct link between the self-sufficiency of the modern self, the rise of anthropocentrism and the ecological crisis[119].

The Technocratic paradigm, that nature is a machine to be exploited, is founded upon an egotistical anthropocentric world view. What-is-more an unqualified reliance on technology as a source of salvation is a modern form of idolatry, the twenty first century version of the molten calf (Exodus 32:4). This type of utilitarian approach to nature causes division between nations. Pope Francis devotes Chapter Three of *Laudato Si'* to the human roots of the ecological crisis and calls for a new paradigm and anthropology. A solution to the modern ecological crisis demands a reassessment and correction of our self-understanding. Elizabeth A. Johnson reminds readers of how Christian Theology, in the first 1500 years, encouraged a positive attitude towards the natural order and points to the reformation as the point of divergence between science and theology. Christianity traditionally is anti-anthropocentric and teaches a move away from self-centeredness to reality centeredness. We only realize our true selves in a decentred relationship with

---

[116] F.L. Cross (ed.) and E.A. Livingston (ed.), *The Oxford Dictionary of the Christian Church*, Oxford, 1983, p. 351.

[117] Dermot A. Lane, *Theology and Ecology in Dialogue: The Wisdom of Laudato Si'*, Dublin, Messenger Publications, 2020, p. 34.

[118] Ibid.

[119] Ibid.

others. The 'Other' includes not only the human other but also the divine other and according to Paul F. Knitter, the earth 'Other'[120].

Pope Benedict XVI wrote extensively about the moral nature of the ecological crisis and about the urgent need for a more human ecology. He acknowledges the crisis is the result of an 'interior desertification taking place within humanity', i.e., it is a moral crisis. In his message for the celebration of the Fortieth World Day of Peace he makes a direct connection between natural ecology, respect for nature, human ecology, and the respect for the dignity of humanity. According to his message, peace itself is founded upon respect for the natural law and respect for the rights of all people. Quoting from *Centesimus Annus*, Pope Benedict XVI emphasised creation is a gift from God that needs to be respected and used for its original purpose. Disregard for the environment harms human coexistence and vice versa[121]. He makes a very valid point acknowledging the connection between peace with creation and peace with men. When we take advantage of the natural world and disrupt the natural order it often leads to conflict between nations. He uses the problem of energy supplies and the race for available resources to illustrate the connection between natural ecology and human ecology. The destruction of the environment and the hoarding of resources can cause grievances between nations due to the inhumane consequences. As we stated previously often what we have termed 'development' is not authentic development because it is unsustainable and often is one nation supressing and exploiting another. For development to be considered integral we need to consider the moral-religious dimension and not limit development to the economic-technical dimension.

---

[120] Paul F. Knitter, Deep Ecumenicity versus Incommensurability: Finding Common Ground on a Common Earth, in Dieter D. Hessel (ed) and Rosemary Radford Ruether (ed), Chr*istianity and Ecology*, Massachusetts, Harvard University Press, 2000, p.378.

[121] Pope Benedict XVI, *Message of his Holiness Pope Benedict XVI For the Celebration of World Day of Peace: The Human Person, The Heart of Peace*, (The Holy See: Papal Archive 2007) 40th World Day of Peace 2007, The Human Person, the Heart of Peace | BENEDICT XVI (vatican.va).

The need for a human ecology is an 'imperative need' [122]. One of the ways to develop an authentic human ecology is through the rediscovery and redefinition of our relationship with the natural environment. The youth are becoming leaders in this field as they remind us our present relationship with nature is disordered. Greta Thunberg states… "Solving the climate crisis is the greatest and most complex challenge *Homo sapiens* have ever faced. The main solution is so simple that even a small child can under-stand it. We must stop our emissions of green-house gases"[123]. The creator has instilled an inbuilt order in creation. We respect this order when we use the fruits of creation responsibly, respecting the natural balance, to satisfy our legitimate needs. We presently are refashioning God given resources into products and ignoring that matter is not just raw material for us to shape at will. The Christian vision sees nature as more than just a raw material we can manipulate for our pleasure. The earth has its own dignity and the universe its own integrity. Respecting the integrity of the universe is the key to discovering our own dignity and freedom. Man can only achieve true freedom through the realization he is not only intellect and will but also nature. Through respecting and listening to his nature man's will becomes rightly ordered as he accepts, he did not create himself. This leads humankind to a loving dependence upon God the '*Creator Spiritus*'[124].

Authentic development will consider our duties arising from our relationship to the natural environment. The current model of global development is incapable of effectively promoting integral human development because it is not inspired by values of human solidarity, charity, and truth[125]. Integral human development will

---

[122] Pope Benedict XVI, *Address of His Holiness Benedict XVI to Six New Ambassadors Accredited to the Holy See,* (The Holy See: Papal Archive, 2011) To the new Ambassadors accredited to the Holy See on the occasion of the presentation of the Letters of Credence (June 9, 2011) | BENEDICT XVI (vatican.va).

[123] Greta Thunberg, *No One is too Small to Make a Difference*, London, Penguin Books, 2019, p.21.

[124] Pope Benedict XVI, *Visit to the Bundestag, Address of his Holiness Benedict XVI: The Listening Heart, Reflections on the Foundations of Law,* (The Holy See: Papal Archive, 2011), Apostolic Journey to Germany: Visit to the Federal Parliament in the Reichstag Building (Berlin, 22 September 2011) | BENEDICT XVI (vatican.va).

[125] Pope Benedict XVI, *Letter of His Holiness Benedict XVI To Hon. Mr Silvio Berlusconi, Prime Minister of Italy, On the Occasion of the G8 Summit,* (The Holy See: Papal Archive,

give a voice to every nation and not only developed countries. Integral human development takes into consideration our responsibility to the poor when making use of the earth's resources and it is marked with solidarity and ensures intergenerational justice[126]. This will only be achieved when we have a vision of creation that sees nature as the setting for our life. It also requires a change in attitude to see nature as representing the love of the Creator for humanity and the *cosmos* as the wonderful result of God's creative activity.

In modern culture any advancement which gives us more control to manipulate the natural world is considered positive. However, often the moral framework to evaluate advancements is inadequate. In the post-modern era nature itself has become a rival for God as human life is placed within the context of ecology and evolution. Elizabeth Johnson recommends returning to early Christian attitudes and teaching as one way to address the modern ills. Christianity will help us to contextualise the universe however there is a need for us to rethink anthropomorphism i.e. the way in which we attribute human characteristics to God. Modern man is anthropocentric, and this permeates every aspect of modern cultures. This affects our image of God as we imagine God to be a cosmic person. This sentiment is echoed by Gordan D. Kaufman as he recommends it is necessary to deconstruct the basic anthropocentrism founded upon our received images and concepts of God to build a genuine relationship with the divine. For example, when we re-imagine God as 'serendipitous creativity'[127] then creation becomes

---

2009), Letter to Hon. Mr. Silvio Berlusconi, President of the Italian Council of Ministers, on the occasion of the G8 Summit [L'Aquila, 8-10 July 2009] (July 1, 2009) | BENEDICT XVI (vatican.va).

[126] Pope Benedict XVI, *Caritas In Veritate: To Bishops, Priests and Deacons, Men and Women Religious, Lay Faithful, And all People of Good Will On Integral Human Development In Charity and Truth*, (The Holy See: Papal Archive, 2009), Caritas in veritate (June 29, 2009) | BENEDICT XVI (vatican.va).

[127] Gordan G. Kaufman, 'Response to Elizabet A. Johnson', in Dieter D. Hessel (ed) and Rosemary Radford Ruether (ed), Chri*stianity and Ecology*, Massachusetts, Harvard University Press, 2000, p.27.

an ongoing process. This is more appropriate to today's ecological understanding of human interconnectedness with nature[128].

When we understand the crisis as a moral crisis within humanity then we begin to reorientate ourselves toward the divine and place the crisis within an established moral framework. Such a framework does not exist within the modern attitude of egotistical anthropocentrism. We do find such a framework within the Judeo-Christian theology of the Cosmos[129]. The Judeo-Christian theology understands that it is our relationship with God that conditions our relationship with the environment[130]. Our understanding of the theological meaning of creation causes us to attribute a moral status to non-human life. When we attribute moral status to non-human life then violence towards non-humanity is deemed to be divergent and sinful. This is an important aspect of Judeo-Christian tradition were, the goodness of creation is emphasized, and according to Nash, the moral status of nature can and must be seen to dwell at the very heart of Christianity[131]. This is what defines us as Christians, our belief that the *cosmos* itself is an expression of God's creative and redemptive purpose for humanity.

There are several implications when we attribute moral status to the non-human world. This view is not without opposition. Many scholars, such as Luc Ferry for example, find it absurd and an opposition to modernity when we attribute moral status to non-human life. He believes concern for non-human life may be addressed within an anthropocentric framework. He disagrees with the attribution of legal subject status to non-human life as this implies a relationship based on reciprocity and recognition of the integral

---

[128] Gordan G. Kaufman, 'Response to Elizabet A. Johnson', in Dieter D. Hessel (ed) and Rosemary Radford Ruether (ed), Chr*istianity and Ecology*, Massachusetts, Harvard University Press, 2000, p.26.

[129] Paul Haffner, *Mystery of Creation*, Herefordshire, Gracewing, 1995, p. 290-291.

[130] Pope John Paul II, *Message of his Holiness pope John Paul II for the Celebration of World Day of Peace: peace with God the Creator, Peace with all of Creation*, [website], 1990, XXIII World Day for Peace 1990,Peace with God the Creator, peace with all of creation | John Paul II (vatican.va), (accessed 29th November 2020).

[131] Daniel Cowdin, 'The Moral Status of Other Kind in Christian Ethics', in Dieter T. Hessel and Rosemary Radford Ruether, *Christianity and Ecology*, Cambridge Massachusetts, Harvard University Press, 2000. p 268.

value of the non-human world. This is not to attribute personhood to non-persons, rather it is to consider if non-persons warrant moral consideration by persons[132]. Luc Ferry obviously adopts the anthropocentric approach placing humanity at the centre of the *cosmos*. He fails to recognize the integrity of creation and its intrinsic value. When we acknowledge nature possesses a value then there are moral implications in our actions towards the environment. Christianity teaches that the moral status of non-human life is related to the theological meaning of creation. The goodness of creation is a common theme throughout the Old Testament to the Patristic Fathers. This concept continued to the Middle Ages as part of what Louis Dupré refers to as the "ontotheological synthesis"[133]. Even empirical science testifies to the *telos* within animals and the ecosystem. If we attribute a moral status to nonhuman life, and we exploit it in any way, we deny its finitude and commit a sin. This in turn has implications for our salvation. The traditional origins of the concept of ecological sin may be traced back to the Old Testament and the Garden of Eden (Genesis 3:6). When we understand sin as insatiable greed that causes us to both take what we want and want to have it all then exploitation of the environment finds its roots in the original sin by the first humans. It is the desire to be God that causes ecological degradation.

The Brazilian ecofeminist theologian Ivone Gebara explained this concept in another way. For Ivone Gebara, the primal sin is not the disobedience that caused us to fall into amorality to which we were not originally subjected, rather the primal sin lies in the effort to escape from mortality, finitude, and vulnerability[134]. Therefore, the source of the ecological crisis is the denial of our vulnerability and mortality causing us to construct exploitative systems to dominate our fellow man and ecosystem. As in the Garden of Eden, modern consumerist lifestyles are taking from the earth's resources to

---

[132] Daniel Cowdin, 'The Moral Status of Other Kind in Christian Ethics', in Dieter T. Hessel and Rosemary Radford Ruether, *Christianity and Ecology*, Cambridge Massachusetts, Harvard University Press, 2000. p 263.

[133] Ibid.

[134] Rosemary Radford Ruether, 'Ecofeminism: The Challenge to Theology', in Dieter T. Hessel and Rosemary Radford Ruether, *Christianity and Ecology*, Cambridge Massachusetts, Harvard University Press, 2000. p 105.

transcend our finite limitations. The system of domination is a type of wizardry, not priestly, and therefore sinful. To understand this concept, we need to broaden our concept sin. Our concept of sin not only includes antisocial acts committed against our fellow human beings and against God but should also include offences against the environment. The Old Testament links human and non-human creatures in the fall and judgment. It is due to the fall in the Garden of Eden that creation is in bondage and both human and non-human creation are in need liberation. The Flood event is an example of how the Earth maybe corrupted (Gen. 6:1-7). Therefore, all of creation, not only humanity needs to be reorientated (Isaiah 11). In the New Testament St. Paul links both material creation (*ktsis*) and humanity in the redemption of Christ (Romans 8:18-23). There is solidarity between the human world and the non-human world in their mutual striving toward a *cosmic* common goal.

When we include non-human creation in our moral vision then this leads us to strive for ecological justice and highlights the need for reconciliation at a personal level and between nations. Our response may be twofold. The first is to challenge the injustice of the internationalization of environmental costs. The second step is to contribute to alternative models of creation and provide guidelines and limitations to our interactions with non-human creation[135]. The internationalization of environmental costs disproportionately effects less industrialized countries as 80% of the earth's resources are consumed by 20% of the earth's population. The WCC statement to the Kyoto Climate Summit in 1997 defined justice as being responsible for one's actions. When we apply this to environmental costs then the bigger the carbon foot print the bigger the moral duty i.e., the bigger the platform the bigger the responsibility[136]. The Council stated that the rich are responsible for the human-produced climate change yet are unwilling to accept the responsibility and translate it into action. An essential element of eco-justice will be honouring promises made in climate agreements. It means being

---

[135] Louke Van Wensveen, 'Christian Ecological Virtue Ethics: Transforming a Tradition', in Dieter T. Hessel and Rosemary Radford Ruether, *Christianity and Ecology*, Cambridge Massachusetts, Harvard University Press, 2000. p 160.

[136] Greta Thunberg, *No One is Too Small to Make a Difference*, London, Penguin Books, 2019, p. 24.

responsible for suffering caused to minorities and being accountable for abuse of power. It also means that the Earth's resources are to be shared equally between all nations. Rich nations need to be truthful and honest about their delinquent actions. They seem to be above the law in relation to international obligations to climate change. The World Council of Churches recommended three confidence building measures to reduce the threat of climate change. The first is for industrialized countries to demonstrate real and significant reductions in domestic greenhouse gas emissions. The second is for developing countries to be more energy-efficient and to limit greenhouse gas emissions. The third is a cross training between the northern hemisphere and the southern hemisphere where the northern hemisphere share their financial and technological resources and the southern hemisphere, specifically indigenous cultures, and women's organisations, offer lessons and tools for learning to live in a socially just, equitable and ecological sustainable manner[137].

If we examine the Paris Climate agreement in 2015, we find the same aspirations. The agreement is based on economic and social transformation. Countries submit their plans for climate action, known as nationally determined contributions (NDCs), every five years and submit long-term low greenhouse gas emission development strategies (LT-LEDS). The countries communicate in the NDCs the actions they will take to build resilience and adapt to the impact of rising temperatures. The Paris Climate agreement is based on the principles of finance, technology and capacity building where developed countries are to provide financial assistance to vulnerable countries to help with mitigation. It speaks of a vision of realizing a technology development and transfer to improve resilience and reduce emissions. The Paris Agreement emphasizes the need for climate-related capacity-building for developing countries and ensures its members increased transparency will be essential to achieve these goals[138].

---

[137] UNFCCC Executive Secretary, Third Session of the Conference of the Parties, [website], 1997, COP 3 | UNFCCC, (accessed 8th January 2021).

[138] UNFCCC Executive Secretary, The Paris Agreement, [website], 2015, The Paris Agreement | UNFCCC, (accessed 8th January 2021).

One positive outcome of the Climate Emergency is countries and disciplines are provided with the opportunity for greater collaboration. It provides richer nations with the opportunity to be reconciled with poorer, vulnerable nations, only when they accept their responsibility for human-induced climate change. From a Christian perspective, respect for the integrity of creation is an essential aspect of the Christian mission. Ecological security will only be achieved through the development of a global culture of ecological responsibility. Our response needs to be personal, political, social, and economic. When we accept the moral dimension of the crisis then we begin to see the external degradation as a symptom of a deep spiritual crisis within humanity.

The moral argument for caring for the environment is made, not only by religious leaders, but by people with political backgrounds. For example, Vice President Al Gore when he was a US senator, stated that he believed at the heart of the environmental crisis is a spiritual crisis. This echoed the belief of the pontiffs that at the heart of the environmental crisis is obviously a moral crisis, a type of soul sickness which increases the suffering of the poor. What is more, we have the moral obligation not to damage the environment for future generations. Pope John Paul II wrote in *Christifideles*, humanity has in its possession a gift that must be passed on to future generations, if possible, passed on in better condition...

> Even these future generations are recipients of the Lord's gifts: "The dominion granted to humanity by the creator is not an absolute power, nor can one speak of a freedom to 'use and misuse', or to dispose of things as one pleases. The limitation imposed from the beginning by the Creator himself and expressed symbolically by the prohibition not to 'eat of the fruit of the tree' (*cf*. Gen 2:16-17) shows clearly enough that, when it comes to the natural world, we are subject not only to biological laws, but also to moral ones, which cannot be violated with impunity[139].

The process of ecological conversion must begin with a conversion of the heart. An essential element of this will be the re-

---

[139] Pope John Paul II, *Chritsifideles Laici*, [website], 1988, Christifideles Laici (December 30, 1988) | John Paul II (vatican.va), (accessed 10th January 2021).

assessment of the place of humanity within creation. St. John Paul II's moral vision is based upon dialogue, respect, and solidarity. He calls for a cessation of the destructive rhetoric that has divided peoples, nations, and cultures. The Earth is something all cultures have in common, our common home. When we establish just structures in societies, this will make it will be easier to be morally accountable for the decisions related to the climate crisis. The moral dilemma is causally related to the way we have cut ourselves off from God's plan. This has caused us not to be concerned for our brothers and sisters and for creation[140]. Care for the planetary garden, according to the book of Genesis, is at the core of our faith. Our partnership with God in caring for creation has scriptural roots. It is only after God entrusts this task to humanity that he rests from his acts of creation (Gen 2: 1-3). For this partnership to be successful we need to be humble and in awe of the Creators plan for the universe[141]. We need to reinterpret "dominion", in the book of Genesis, as *dominus* in Latin meaning 'to be of the Lord'.

---

[140] Pope John Paul II, *Message of John Paul II for the 23rd World Day of Tourism 2002*, [website], 2002, Message for World Tourism Day (September 27, 2002) | John Paul II (vatican.va), (accessed 10th January 2022).

[141] Marybeth Lorbiecki, *Following St. Francis: John Paul II's call for Ecological Action*, New York, Rizzoli ex libris, 2014, p. 46.

Scripture and Ecology

Old Testament

One important source of the Judeo-Christian attitude toward creation is the Scriptures. An exegesis of scriptural passages from both the Old and the New Testament will clarify any ambiguity in the text related to the goodness of the natural world. Overall, the Scriptures portrays a positive view of the universe. Richard Bauckham refers to the Genesis account of creation as being 'ecological'[142]. The first book of the Pentateuch, Genesis is divided into two parallel sections. The first describes through narrative, the origin of the nations and how God created the world (Genesis 1:1 – 11:26). The Hebrew words used to describe the earth as formless and void, *tōhû wābōhû*, suggest the earth is entirely covered with water and uninhabitable by humans. The Spirit moving over the water is described as the wind of God. The Hebrew word used here, *rûah,* describes air in motion and may be translated as wind, breath, and spirit. This is one of the most used terms for spirit in the Jewish Bible. The term is found in 378 places and it is impossible to capture the uniqueness of Judaism without reference to *rûah[143]*. The creative spirit of God is a leitmotif running through Genesis one and two. The Church fathers interpreted the spirit in Genesis to be Holy Spirit.

In the book of Genesis, creation is the immediate result of the word of God. The concept of *Logos* in the Judeo-Christian tradition provides the sense God comes to us as an utterance[144]. Both the Word

---

142 Richard Bauckham, *Bible and Ecology,* London, Darton Longman and Todd, 2010, p. 15.

143 Dermot A. Lane, *Theology and Ecology in Dialogue: The Wisdom of Laudato Si'*, Dublin, Messenger Publications, p.63.

144 Paul Ricoeur, *Interpretation Theory: Discourse and the Surplus of Meaning*, Fort Worth, Texas University Press, 1976, cited in Dieter T. Hessel (ed.) and Rosemary Radford

65

of God and the Wisdom of God participate in the work of creation and are intrinsic to the divine identity. Jewish monotheism emphasised God carried out the work of creation solely by means of his own word. In the book of Wisdom, the creative Word of God is identified with Wisdom (Wisdom 9:1) and in the book of Sirach the Lords works are done by his words (Si 42:15).

According to Elizabeth Johnson behind every line about the *Logos* there lies the story of Wisdom[145]. Wisdom knows the changes of the seasons, the movements of animals, the healing properties of herbs and renews all things with a life-giving energy[146]. The book of Proverbs recalls how the Wisdom of God existed before creation (Proverbs 8: 22-26). Wisdom's superiority over all things is due to her pre-existence before all created things. In the book of Wisdom, Wisdom herself is the unerring source of rational knowledge (Wisdom 7: 17-21). Creation itself is dependent upon the will of God (Wisdom 11:25). Richard Bauckham writes, "Both the Word and the Wisdom of God take part in the work of creation, sometimes with distinguishable roles, sometimes interchangeably"[147].

In Genesis 1:1, known as the *opus creationis*, God's action is the sole principle through which the elements of the Universe are created[148]. All of creation has a dependency upon God who pre-exists creation. This is echoed in Isaiah 44: 24 where God alone is the creator of the entire cosmos. God creates out of nothing and not from pre-existent material. Belief in creation *ex nihilo* is mentioned for the first time in 2 Maccabees 7:28. The Jewish woman's exhortation to her Son expresses the climate of thought in Israel implicit in Genesis Chapter 1... "I beg you, my child, to look at the heaven and the earth and see everything that is in them and recognise God did not make them out of things that existed. Thus, also mankind comes into

---

Ruether (ed.), *Christianity and Ecology Seeking the Wellbeing of Earth and Humans,* Cambridge Massachusetts, Harvard University Press, 2000, p. 318.

[145] Dermot A. Lane, *Theology and Ecology in Dialogue: The Wisdom of Laudato Si'*, Dublin, Messenger Publications, p.77.

[146] Elizabeth A. Johnson, *Losing and Finding Creation in the Christian Tradition,* in Dieter T. Hessel and Rosemary Radford Ruether, *Christianity and Ecology,* Cambridge Massachusetts, Harvard University Press, 2000. p 5.

[147] Richard Bauckham, J*esus, and the God of Israel*, Milton Keynes, Paternoster, 2008, p.16.

[148] Paul Haffner, *Mystery of Creation,* Herefordshire, Gracewing, 2010, p. 66.

being". This is contrary to the human experience of creating from pre-existent material. The Judeo-Christian tradition of *creatio ex nihilio* contrasts with the teaching of Aristotle who taught that the world was not created but had existed for all eternity. The first three days of creation are marked with creation of environments and names. God separates the light and darkness creating day and night, firmament is separated from waters creating sky and dry land separated from the waters creating land sea and vegetation. In day four five and six the environments are inhabited with heavenly lights, creatures in the water, sky, and land. The pinnacle of God's creation occurs on day six with the creation of humanity. Yahweh makes the decision to create humanity in his image and likeness, *Imago Dei.*

St. Gregory Nyssa identifies the *Imago* with human free will. This is derived from the anthropomorphic expression in Genesis 1:26 indicating divine freedom in creation[149]. St. Augustine understands *Imago Dei* in Trinitarian terms with the image of the Trinity found in the intellectual nature of the soul in the three powers of memory representing the Father, intellect representing the Son, and will representing the Holy Spirit. The freedom of God's creation is emphasized by the Church throughout the centuries. For example, the Council of Sens (1140) condemned several of the writings of Peter Abelard (1079-1142) for denying God's freedom in creation. *Lumen Gentium* states ... "The plan of the eternal Father's wisdom and goodness is utterly free; it is his secret: he created the whole world, decided to raise men to a share in the divine life"[150]. In both the Churches of the East and the Churches of the West the fact that we are made *Imago Dei* makes it possible to enter union with God "*capax Dei*". Pope John Paul II writes God opens himself up to man in his spirit and man is created as a subject capable of accepting divine self-communication...

> Man – as the tradition of Christian thought maintains – is "capax Dei": capable of knowing God and of receiving the gift he makes of himself. Indeed, created in the image and likeness of God (cf. *Gn* 1:26), he is able to live a personal

---

[149] Paul Haffner, *Mystery of Creation*, Herefordshire, Gracewing, 2010, p. 79.

[150] Vatican Council II, *Lumen Gentium on the Church*, London, Catholic Truth Society, 2004.

relationship with him and to respond with loving obedience to the covenant relationship offered to him by is creator[151].

The intrinsic goodness of the created elements is emphasised six times in Genesis and climatically a seventh time of the entire universe (Genesis 1:31). The ontological goodness of creation is a divine pronouncement and not a deduction from human experience. Each stage of creation is appreciated for its own sake and the goodness of each stage of creation is reaffirmed with a refrain. The Old Testament cosmogony differs from the Near eastern cosmogonies of the Sumerians, Babylonians, and the Assyrians in the emergence of a Sabbath day of rest. In the Old Testament Sabbath exists because of the perfection and goodness of God's work. The practice of Sabbath and of Jubilee when the animals rest and the land is refreshed by lying fallow, in the Deuteronomic tradition, give a concrete expression to the way in which creation is an intrinsic part of the community's religious worship and practice[152].

The longest passages in the Old Testament related to non-human creation may be found in the book of Job (Job 38, 39). They are what may be referred to as theopoetic and are characterised by their appreciation of wild nature. God, the all-powerful and all-wise ruler of nature and history, answers Job's question out of a whirlwind. God invites Job to a vast panorama of the *cosmos* and reorders Job's whole view of the world. Job is placed in his cosmic place[153]. The ten strophes indicate God is the cosmic architect controlling the cosmic order. God regulates because he knows. Job has no power to control because he does not know, and the effect is cosmic humility at knowing only God is God. Job shifts from an anthropocentric vision of the cosmos to a decentred theocentric vision of the *cosmos* is an example to modern man.

---

[151] Pope John Paul II, *General Audience*, [website], 1998, http://www.vatican.va/content/john-paul-ii/en/audiences/1998/documents/hf_jp-ii_aud_26081998.html, (accessed 27th September 2020).

[152] Elizabeth A. Johnson, *Losing and Finding Creation in the Christian Tradition*, in Dieter T. Hessel and Rosemary Radford Ruether, *Christianity and Ecology*, Cambridge Massachusetts, Harvard University Press, 2000. p. 5.

[153] Richard Bauckham, *Bible and Ecology*, London, Darton Longman and Todd, 2010, p. 39.

The Psalmists' approach to nature gives us an insight into the Jewish connection with the land and their dependence on soils and weather. The Psalmists' particularly give us an appreciation of the weather through a countryman's eyes[154]. For example, the sending of rain at the beginning of the agricultural years is indicative of God's benevolence to Israel (Psalm 65: 9-14). God's goodness is measured in the abundance of rain and food as drought is the result of sin making confession and repentance necessary. As the Hebrews believed in one God there is a clear distinction between nature, God's creation, and God the creator of heaven and Earth. The entire universe, and the conditions of time and space, are produced through the freewill of a perfect, timeless, unconditioned God who is above and outside of all that he makes. Judaic thought brings both nature and God into relation and separates them. When nature is emptied of its divinity it becomes an index, a manifestation of the Divine[155]. For example, when we read Psalm 36: 5-6, images of height and depth are magnificent symbols of Divinity because the natural objects are no longer taken themselves to be divine. Nature becomes full of manifestations showing the presence of God (Psalm 29: 3-5). Nature is portrayed by the Psalmists' as being an awesome achievement of God. Its permanence is evidence of his faithfulness (Psalm 33: 4-9). Its limitations are by design (Psalm 148:6).

New Testament

Bible scholars make a direct connection between the *Wisdom of God (sophia)* in the Old Testament, and the Word of God, *Logos*, in the New Testament. Raymond Brown describes Jesus as the culmination of a tradition that runs through the Wisdom literature of the Old Testament[156]. The microcosm of creation, which reached its pinnacle with the creation of humanity in Genesis 1 and 2, reaches a climax in the New Testament with the Christ event. There are echoes

---

[154] C.S. Lewis, *Reflections on the Psalms*, London, William Collins, 1958, p. 90.

[155] Ibid., p. 93-95.

[156] Raymond Brown, *The Gospel According to John*, New York, Doubleday, 1966, cited in Dermot A. Lane, *Theology and Ecology in Dialogue: The Wisdom of Laudato Si'*, Dublin, Messenger Publication, 2020, p. 77.

of the creation event in Genesis one in the Christological hymn contained in John 1: 1-18. The *Logos Christology* in John's prologue recounts the decent of the eternal word into human history enabling humans to partake of divine fulness[157]. John exceeds the wisdom tradition of the Old Testament suggesting there is equality between wisdom and God. The Word becoming flesh (sarx) goes beyond *Wisdom* dwelling within Israel in Exodus 25: 8-9. The celebration of the pre-existent word of God connects Christology to the theme of creation in the sapiential Bible literature and bridges the dialogue between ecology and Christology[158]. The incarnation is necessitated by the rejection of divine wisdom by humanity. Ironically, Christ the true light is rejected by his own (John 1: 10-11).

Dermot A. Lane elaborates on four parallels between the *Logos* in John's Gospel and the figure of *Wisdom* in the Hebrew Bible. Firstly, *Wisdom* existed in the beginning with God (Prov. 8:22-23) just as the *Logos* existed in the beginning (John 1:1). *Wisdom* is the pure emanation of the Glory of the Almighty (Prov. 8:17:5) and the *Logos* in John reveals the Glory of God (John 1:14). *Wisdom*, in the Old Testament, reflects the everlasting light of God (Wisdom 7:26), whereas in John's Gospel the light of the *Logos* is the light of the World (John 1: 4-5). *Wisdom* in the Old Testament is described as having descended from heaven to dwell with the people (Sirach 24:8) whereas in John the *Logos* descended from heaven to Earth (John 1:14)[159]. The theme of Christ as the *Wisdom* of God is recurring in the writings of St. Paul. In Colossians 1:15-20 the role of Christ in creation alludes to the *Wisdom* motifs in the Old Testament. He is given the role previously given to the figure of *Wisdom* in the Old Testament. His pre-existence reflects the *Wisdom* speculation in Hellenistic Judaism[160]. He is present at the beginning of all things.

---

[157] Pheme Perkins, *The Gospel According to John,* in Raymond E. Brown, Joseph A. Fitzmyer, Roland E. Murphy (ed.), *The New Jerome Biblical Commentary,* London, Geoffrey Chapman, 1990, p. 943.

[158] Dermot A. Lane, *Theology and Ecology in Dialogue: The Wisdom of Laudato Si',* Dublin, Messenger Publications, 2020, p. 79.

[159] Ibid., p. 77-78.

[160] Mauyra P. Horgan, *The Letter to The Colossians,* in Raymond E. Brown, Joseph A. Fitzmyer, Roland E. Murphy (ed.), *The New Jerome Biblical Commentary,* London, Geoffrey Chapman, 1990, p. 879.

There are further examples of biblical parallels between the Old and the New Testament in the synoptic Gospel's. Luke uses the Greek word *epeskioso* (Luke 1:35) to describe the Spirit overshadowing Mary, the same word used in Genesis for the Spirit moving over the waters (Genesis 1:2) This signifies Christ, the new creation, is a pure Gift of God and incarnated through the power of the Spirit. The Nativity scene in the New Testament is depicted as a reversal of earthly kingship (Luke 2: 1-7). Christ is not depicted as being surrounded by human retainers, rather he is surrounded by adoring animals. Christ is placed at the centre of the *cosmos*. The New Testament places Christ at the centre of all of creation as through the incarnation God enters the suffering of all and obtains redemption for all through Christ's life death and resurrection.

The many frescos, mosaics and sarcophagi created in the first centuries after the emergence of Christian texts are helpful in gauging early Christian Churches attitude toward creation. Although the first catacomb painters did not portray the creation event, Adam and Eve often appear in the Garden of Eden surrounded with animals and plants. The Christian Catacombs are decorated with pastoral scenes closely related to the environment including evergreen vegetation and blooming flowers. Belief in the resurrection is symbolised with the ever-renewing nature motif[161]. The central position of the image of 'Jesus the good shepherd' (John 10:11) in ceiling after ceiling in the Christian catacombs projects virtues such as conscientious citizenship and care for others[162]. The Good Shepherd's innocence and lack of worldly malice, as evidenced by his purse, pipes, and bucket of sheep's milk, is an inversion of worldly power and authority (see figure 1). The Good Shepherd is surrounded with images from nature such as trees, herbs, and birds as displayed in the Catacomb of Domitilla. Early Christian frescos often depict a personification of the seasons around the Good Shepherd. The Good shepherd is a symbol for Christian leadership. He interacts, not with another, person but with greater creation. When the good shepherd is

---

[161]Susan P. Bratton, 'Anti-Imperial Themes and Care for Living Nature in Early Christian Art: The Good Shepherd as a Model for Christian Environmental Ethics' in Kyle S. Van Houtan (ed) and Michael S. Northcott (ed), *Diversity and Dominion*, Oregon, Cascade Books, 2010, p.115.

[162] Ibid., p.116.

depicted with a dog, the dog looks toward the master waiting for a command. The dog, when depicted, symbolizes the virtues of a disciplined Christian who is patient, protective, loyal, gentle, and courageous. The Good Shepherd also symbolizes the attractiveness of Christ to all of creation and represents the divine intention for nature. The image of the Good Shepherd from the early Church gives us a model of creation care. The sheep on his shoulders represents both the soul of a Christian and the biosphere on which we depend. He provides a glimpse of God's kingdom where peace extends to all creation. Susan P. Braton writes... "If we refrain from greed and hubris, and the other indifferent excesses of human control, and, instead, join the Shepherd in simple caretaking, God's blessing will flow unhindered and the greatest artwork of all, the creation, will retain its beauty and diversity until the end of days"[163].

Christ the Good Shepherd based on statuettes of Hermes. The Good shepherd is a friend and caretaker for the living earth. He is portrayed as youthful, wearing simple landsman clothes, and accompanied or carrying animals. Location: Museo Pio Cristiano, Vatican Museums, Vatican State[164].

The Place of Humanity in Creation

The microcosm of creation begins in Genesis Chapter 1 verses 26 and 27 with the creation of humanity. In the spatial scheme of creation there is no sense of a progressive evolution of increasing intelligence and complexity resulting in humanity. Rather, humanity is an integral part of the of an independent whole. Humanity is the

---

[163] Susan P. Bratton, 'Anti-Imperial Themes and Care for Living Nature in Early Christian Art: The Good Shepherd as a Model for Christian Environmental Ethics' in Kyle S. Van Houtan (ed) and Michael S. Northcott (ed), *Diversity and Dominion*, Oregon, Cascade Books, 2010, p.128.

[164] Scala Art Resources NY, 'Good Shepherds', first half of fourth Century, in in Kyle S. Van Houtan (ed) and Michael S. Northcott (ed), *Diversity and Dominion*, Oregon, Cascade Books, 2010, p.129.

apex of God's creation (Gn 1:31) representing the unity of body and soul. It is the creative difference between man and woman which makes humanity *Imago Dei*. Unlike the other creatures we are imprinted with the natural law and participate in the divine plan for the *cosmos*. The breath of God, *pneuma*, within humanity is what makes man spiritual and material (Gn 2:7). Genesis 1: 26-27, where God gives mankind dominion over creation, has often been misinterpreted and used as a justification for humanities unbridled exploitation of the earth and its resources. Paul Haffner writes… "Far from encouraging an unbridled and anthropocentric exploitation of the natural environment, the theology behind *Imago Dei* affirms man's crucial role in the realization of God's eternal abiding in the perfect universe. Human beings are by design administrators of this transformation in which all of creation yearns"[165]. In the Jewish sense 'dominion' is understood as caring, protecting, overseeing, and preserving. There is no evidence in the text to support the belief that creation was created only for use by humanity. This justifies a reassessment of the dominion model of creation. The Jewish word for dominion, *radah*, when used with land, *eretz,* as an object has a meaning more like possession and cultivation. The same meaning is found in other Old Testament passages where the land is entrusted to the Israelites as part of the Covenant however the land belongs to the Lord (Lv. 25:23)[166]. The dominion model of Creation is rejected by Christians in favour of the stewardship model. The stewardship model finds its origins in Genesis 2:15 where Adam is tasked with tilling and keeping the earth.

In Genesis three, the harmony of God's creation begins to break down. The temptation to be like God, and the original sin of disobedience causes disharmony between body and soul, man and woman, human person and creation, and humanity and God. The disobedience of God's command, not to eat from the tree of knowledge in the Garden of Eden, causes the fall of humanity. This results in the loss of original innocence and eventual expulsion from Eden. Man forgets his unique place within creation. Original sin expresses itself in violence as the first homicide is recorded in

---

[165] Paul Haffner, *Mystery of Creation,* Herefordshire, Gracewing, 2010, p. 116.

[166] Richard Bauckham, *Bible and Ecology,* London, Darton Longman and Todd, 2010, p.17.

Genesis 4:8 when Cain kills his brother Abel. Richard Bauckham writes of humanity …

> Their taking possession of the Earth has actually filled the earth with violence. Instead of an appropriately limited use of the Earth's resources, humans have over-exploited the Earth, with the result that they engage in violent competition among themselves, they deprive wild animals of their food, and both humans and animals resort to meat-eating[167].

The role of humanity according to the Scriptures is to care for creation. Human beings have a role beyond compare within creation. Humanity has the responsibility to communicate with nature as an intelligent and noble master and guardian and not its heedless exploiter and destroyer[168]. This responsibility includes ensuring the common destination and equitable distribution of the Earth's resources.

---

[167] Richard Bauckham, *Bible and Ecology,* London, Darton Longman and Todd, 2010, p.24.

[168] Pope John Paul II, *Redemptor Hominis*, [website], 1979, Redemptor Hominis (4 March 1979) | John Paul II (vatican.va), (accessed 7th March 2021).

Ecology and the Development of Catholic Social Teaching

The Development of Catholic Social Teaching

The main vehicles for Catholic Social teaching on the environment have been the Roman Catholic Magisterium, the constitutions, decrees, and declarations issued at Ecumenical Councils, direct Papal teaching issued as encyclicals, teaching from Episcopal Conferences e.g. CELAM (Latin American Bishops Conference), and insights from ecumenical dialogue. Each have created a backdrop for the publication of *Laudato Si'*, the encyclical published in 2015 devoted completely to ecological conversion. Pope Francis' twenty-one references to documents of episcopal conferences is a testimony to his acute sense of collegiality and synodality and his recognition of the importance of previous teaching as building blocks. The documents of the ecumenical councils carry the highest weight. Next will be the Papal documents such as decretals, encyclical letters, and apostolic exhortations. Episcopal conference documents have lesser weight than the documents of the universal magisterium. Documents addressed to a universal audience will have greater weight than those addressed to a particular group and their reception will affect the determination of their weight. Collegiality is a factor in the potential weight of a document.

Church teaching related to the environment began to gain impetus during the Second Vatican Council. The Council was called by Pope John XXIII who had previously been a Vatican diplomat and had experience in working in countries with small Roman Catholic populations. In *Pacem in Terris* he states that what emerges from scientific knowledge and inventions of technology is the greatness of

God who created both man and the universe[169]. The emphasis is on the disunity among nations in contrast with the order in the universe. Pope John XXIII calls for states to collaborate in order to pool both their material and spiritual resources to work for the common good of the entire human family. Collaboration is imperative if nations are to facilitate the circulation of goods, capital, and manpower[170]. Pope John XXIII expresses his distress at seeing the outlay of intellectual and material resources to stockpile armaments in developed countries while other countries lack help for economic and social development. He states that wealthier nations, though they provide aid for poorer states, must have the highest possible respect for poorer states national characteristics and civil institutions and he repudiates any policy of dominion. The ideal goal is the establishment of a world community of equals and the attainment of universal prosperity. Human resources alone will not achieve this. It is only with God's heavenly assistance that human society can bear the closest possible resemblance to the Kingdom of God. The triad approach of 'See, Judge, Act' is adopted by Pope John XXIII in *Mater et Magistra.* It has its origins in the work of Cardinal Joseph Cardijn (1882-1967) of Belgium who adopted the triad approach to implement the church's social teaching. It is also the method adopted by Pope Francis in *Laudato Si'.*

Paul VI, in *Gaudium et Spes,* discusses anthropologically based themes of human responsibility and the dignity of human work for the common good. He addresses the place and roll of humanity in the universe focusing on the total presentation of man, whole and entire body and soul, heart and conscience, mind and will. He states that humanity enjoys an abundance of wealth, resources, and economic power yet the majority of the world's citizens are tormented by hunger, poverty, and illiteracy. He envisages a day when all of creation will be unchained from the bondage of vanity.

The same themes of the dignity of human work and human responsibility are found in Pope Paul VI's 1967 encyclical *Populorum Progressio.* He states that the progressive development

---

[169] Pope John XXIII, *Pacem In Terris,* [website], 1963, Pacem in Terris (April 11, 1963) | John XXIII (vatican.va), (accessed 17th January 2021).

[170] Ibid.

of all peoples is of interest to the Church. For development to be authentic it must be well rounded, foster the development of each man and the whole of man. Just as all of creation is ordered toward the creator, so too must the rational creature direct his life toward God. Pope Paul VI refers to progress as a 'two-edged sword'[171]. Progress is necessary for man's development, however if he cannot look beyond it to the supreme good then it enslaves him. Men's hearts become hardened when they shut out others from their minds. The lack of a sense of 'otherness' causes mankind to gather for self-interest rather than friendship and this leads only to dissention and disunity. Mankind fills the emptiness within by buying and owning more and more possessions. Consumerism and material possessions prevent mankind from realizing his true vocation. Authentic human development transitions humankind from less than human conditions to truly human conditions. Pope Paul VI outlines three duties of wealthier nations. The first is mutual solidarity with developing nations, the second is social justice between strong and weak nations and the third universal charity. In summary he asks that one standard apply for all nations.

In *Octogesima Adveniens* (1971), Paul VI makes direct reference to the environment (nn. 21). He states that mankind risks destroying nature through ill-considered exploitation and risks becoming a victim of his own degradation[172]. He identifies several factors including the menacing material environment, pollution, refuse, new illness, our destructive capacity, and the uncontrollable human framework, which will create an environment which will be intolerable. What is most interesting in his writings is the almost prophetic statement from Pope Paul VI that this will be a wide-ranging social problem which will concern the entire human family. Our intelligence and capacity to do good increases the Christian responsibility for our common destiny.

---

[171] Pope Paul VI, *Populorum Progressio: Encyclical of Pope Paul VI On the Development of Peoples,* [website], 1967, Populorum Progressio (March 26, 1967) | Paul VI (vatican.va), (accessed 19th January 2021).

[172] Pope Paul VI, Octogesima Adveniens, [website], 1971, Octogesima Adveniens (May 14, 1971) | Paul VI (vatican.va), (accessed 19th January 2021).

In June 1977 Paul VI delivered his message for the Fifth World-Wide day of the Environment. He begins the letter with a quote from Genesis "And God saw everything that he had made, and behold, it was very good" (Gen. 1:31). His message in the opening paragraph is that creation is to be embraced in its totality as good because it is a gift from the creator. Again, we hear the themes of interdependence and solidarity as we are encouraged to live out our vocations in our environment. We even have the effect of ennobling the environment by our presence, work, and contemplation. Pope Paul VI places a strong emphasis on the stewardship of creation as part of the Christian responsibility is to ensure the health of the environment for future generations. The concept that humanity ennobles the environment though our presence and endeavour is an interesting one that deserves further development. By stating this Paul VI reaffirms that we are in our natural habitat and in a certain sense we complete the natural order. The true purpose and beauty of creation and the environment is in some way realized through our presence and through good human activity.

One of the greatest recent social educators, in relation to environmental issues, is Pope John Paul II. There are several reasons for this namely environmental degradation reached critical levels at the end of the last century during his pontificate and continue until present. In many ways he had to address issues related to the environment that did not apply for earlier generations. He addresses environmental issues in five encyclical letters. The first is *Redemptor Hominis* (1979). Here Pope John Paul II references mankind's fear of his ability to be an instrument for self-destruction, through the work of his hands, his intellect and will. The earth is being exploited for industrial and military purposes and technology is developed outside of the framework of a humanistic plan[173]. As a result, man becomes alienated from nature and sees no meaning in the natural environment other than what serves for immediate use and consumption. The Pope correctly points out the dangers in technological advancements without proportional development in morals and ethics. We need to reprioritize developments in ethics and

---

[173] Pope John Paul II, *Redemptor Hominis*, [website], 1979, Redemptor Hominis (4 March 1979) | John Paul II (vatican.va), (accessed 30th January 2021).

morality before developments in technology. He correctly identifies humanities dominating actions as the source of pollution of the natural environment and the source of armed conflicts[174]. His anthropocentric focus in *Redemptor Hominis* is on the dignity of humanity and their responsibility to ensure equal distribution of the earth's resources.

In *Laborem Excercens* (1981), Pope John Paul II, identifies work as the fundamental dimension of the existence of humanity on the earth. He refers to mankind's mandate, based on being made *Imagio Dei,* to subdue and dominate the earth. He explains the concept of dominion in a transitive sense and the command to 'subdue the earth' as being wide ranging. What is important is the Pope sees the relevance of passages from Genesis for today when correctly interpreted. It is through man's work that he confirms dominion over the earth, and this is part of the creators' original design and ordering[175]. The correct way to understand dominion is in the context of the dignity of work. When we do not associate dominion with the concept of the dignity of work then this leads to an exploitative relationship with the natural environment. He identifies two aspects of the biblical concept of 'dominion', the first being the objective dimension of work and the second being the subjective dimension of work. Work, in the objective sense, refers indirectly to man's ability to subdue the earth through the work of his hands. As a person, man is the subject of work performing the actions belonging to the work process independently of their objective content[176]. When man throughout the process confirms himself as the one who dominates and subdues the earth then work corresponds to the biblical concept. It is this subjective understanding of work in nature that is ethical for it presupposes the person who carries out the work is a conscious and free subject. Therefore, the value of human work is determined not so much by the work being done but by the fact that the person doing the work is a person. The dignity of work

---

[174] Kevin W. Irwin, *A Commentary on Laudato Si': Examination the background, Contributions, Implementation, and Future of Pope Francis's Encyclical*, New York, Paulist Press, 2016, p. 15.

[175] Pope John Paul II, *Laborem Exercens*, [website], 1981, Laborem Exercens (14 September 1981) | John Paul II (vatican.va), (accessed 30th January 2021).

[176] Ibid.

is in the subjective understanding as this dispels the differentiation of people into different classes according to the type of work being done. Although the type of work people can do may have greater or lesser objective value the measure of dignity is the person, the subject of work. Pope John Paul II's clarification of the biblical concept of 'dominion' provides us with a healthy attitude toward the earth and its resources. Humanity itself needs to be given priority especially in the mechanisation of tasks as when the machine is exalted it reduces humanity to the status of being a slave. We may only consider the work that we do to be ethical when it makes provision for future generations. In other words, the work we do needs to be sustainable to be considered ethical.

In his encyclical *Sollicitudo Rei Socialis* (1987) John Paul II develops his thought about development and the preservation of the Earth's resources. This encyclical represents a pivotal moment in the Churches discourse on the environment for it is the first time a Church leader expresses concern about the limitation of the earth's resources. He identifies industrialisation as being either directly or indirectly responsible for environmental pollution. This letter focuses on the nature of authentic development. In his opening line, he states that authentic development will promote all the dimensions of the human person. He describes underdevelopment and poverty as the source of grief and anxiety and the underdevelopment of nations as a concern. Throughout the letter he develops the moral dimension of authentic development. For example, true development cannot be considered as the accumulation of wealth and greater availability of goods and services when this is gained at the expense of the development of the masses without considering the social, cultural, and spiritual dimension of the human being[177]. This is evidently an issue of social justice. Our concept of development is often narrowed to the economic one and does not duly affirm the many dimensions of the human person, as success is determined in terms of financial success. True development will result in the fair distribution of the earth's resources thus placing a limit on our dominion of the earth's resources. He advises man his dominion of the earth must remain the

---

[177] Pope John Paul II, *Sollicitudo Rei Socialis*, [website], 1987, Sollicitudo Rei Socialis (30 December 1987) | John Paul II (vatican.va), (accessed 30th January 2021).

subject to the will of God who places limits on his dominion over the things of the earth (Genesis 2: 16-17). Therefore, true development can only consist in subordinating the possession, dominion and use of the earth's resources to man's divine likeness and vocation to be moral[178]. The task of dominion is to be accomplished within the framework of obedience to the divine law. His concept of the limitation of the earth's resources is best expressed by the prohibition in the Garden of Eden not to eat the fruit of the tree (Genesis 2: 16-17). In relation to the natural world there are moral laws which cannot be broken without impunity. The recognition of the limitation of the earth's resources and their subsequent equal allocation between nations is dependent upon good planning.

In *Centesimus Annus* (1991) Pope John Paul II analyses the anthropological error of denying the earth's resources are from God. When we do this and exploit the earth's resources, we deny God's original purpose for creation. He states that in the race to reverse the damage to the natural environment we are forgetting to mention the more serious destruction of the human environment. Human ecology refers to safeguarding the moral conditions in societies to ensure the authentic development of each facet or our being i.e., respect for the natural and moral order. One point deserves further development and that is not only has God gifted the natural world to us, but man is also God's gift to man[179]. This means we should live our vocation in solidarity with each other in this our common home. The first structure of human ecology we encounter is the family where we learn our personhood.

The fifth and final encyclical letter containing environmental teaching from Pope John Paul II, is *Evangelium Vitae* (1995). His main message relates to the dignity of humanity in the order of creation due to our ability to know our creator. Belief in God is essential for man to see himself as mysteriously different from the

---

[178] Pope John Paul II, *Sollicitudo Rei Socialis*, [website], 1987, Sollicitudo Rei Socialis (30 December 1987) | John Paul II (vatican.va), (accessed 30th January 2021).

[179] Pope John Paul II, *Centesimus Annus*, [website], 1991, Centesimus Annus (1 May 1991) | John Paul II (vatican.va), (accessed 30th January 2021).

rest of creation[180]. When we remove the necessity of God it has the effect of distorting nature, reducing it to matter to be manipulated. He questions the way in which we interpret the quality of life. Presently quality of life is measured as economic efficiency, inordinate consumerism, physical beauty, and pleasure. Such a materialistic attitude towards life impoverishes our humanity through the neglect of consideration for our interpersonal, spiritual, and religious dimensions[181]. Citing Genesis 1:28 he describes the task entrusted to mankind as to promote, show reverence for and love life. The concept of having dominion over the earth is understood as a sign of glory and honour from the creator. The main point here is that the 'dominion' granted by the creator is not an absolute power and the freedom to use and misuse. The command from God to 'till the earth and keep it' (Genesis 2:15) is indicative of man's responsibility toward creation. This responsibility is not only to the natural world and the preservation of species but also relates to human ecology. The themes running through the encyclical include the recognition that the ecological question includes human ecology and the symbolic limitation placed by the creator in the beginning not to eat the fruit of the tree of knowledge (Genesis 2: 16-17). This demonstrates clearly the natural world is subject not only to biological laws but also to moral laws.

The first solar panels were installed in the Vatican during the pontificate of Pope Benedict XVI. Known as the 'Green Pope' he frequently wrote on environmental issues. Although we do not have an encyclical letter dealing solely with environmental issues, he provides an abundance of teaching on ecology. For example, in a catechesis during November in 2005 he examines the themes of the covenant and creation as outlined in the Psalm 136[135]. The word *hesed* is used to describe the covenant between God and his people which is characterised by God's mercy and lovingkindness. According to the Psalmist, creation is the first sign of divine love, the second is history. Pope Benedict XVI describes the skies, the earth,

---

[180] Pope John Paul II, *Evangelium Vitae*, [website], 1995, Evangelium Vitae (25 March 1995) | John Paul II (vatican.va), (accessed 3oth January 2021).

[181] Ibid.

the seas, the sun, the moon, the stars as a 'cosmic revelation'[182]. The primacy of creation as a revelation of divine love deserves further consideration as it is a revelation open to all humanity. The Psalms implicitly state that a divine message is secretly engraved in creation. It is the message of *hesed,* of the loving fidelity of the creator who provides for his creation (Psalm 19[18]). When we understand the universe as a cosmic revelation then praise of the Lord will flow from contemplation of his marvellous works. The contemplation of creation will raise our minds to the Lord, his loving mercy, and his creative wisdom. In his homily on the Solemnity of the Body and Blood of Christ in 2006 we find an explicit statement regarding the relationship between the Eucharist and the *cosmos*[183]. Pope Benedict XVI refers to the words of Christ at the Last Supper as the central event of the history of the world and our personal lives[184]. The homily focuses on the bread and wine and how they are a sign of the presence of *Jesus.* The bread and wine are not simply a product of human labour but rather the fruit of the earth and a gift. He states that credit for the fruit of the earth belongs to the creator, for God has made the Earth fertile. Therefore, the gifts at the Eucharist symbolise a synergy between Heaven and Earth. The little white host represents cooperation between Heaven and Earth as this bread of the poor appears as the synthesis of creation[185]. He understands the Eucharist within the context of creation and salvation history. He echoes the words of St. Paul in Romans 8: 18-25 when stating that creation is itself aspiring to something greater. That something greater is his divinisation and unification with the creator. This is realised in the consecration of bread and wine at the Eucharist.

---

[182] Pope Benedict XVI, General Audience, [website], 2005, General Audience of 9 November 2005: Psalm 136[135] - His mercy endures for ever! | BENEDICT XVI (vatican.va), (accessed 31st January 2021).

[183] Kevin W. Irwin, *A Commentary on Laudato Si': Examining the Background, Contributions, Implementation, and Future of Pope Francis' Encyclical*, New York, Paulist Press, 2016, p. 28.

[184] Pope Benedict XVI, *Homily of his Holiness Benedict XVI: Holy Mass and Eucharistic Procession on the Solemnity of the Sacred Body and Blood of Christ*, [website], 2006, 15 June 2006: Solemnity of the Sacred Body and Blood of Christ - Mass and Eucharistic Procession | BENEDICT XVI (vatican.va), (accessed 31st January 2021).

[185] Ibid.

In his address to the Diplomatic Corps accredited to the Holy See he opens by addressing the structural economic dysfunction which is causing the scandal of hunger. This global phenomenon is scandalous because we have the resources to bring it to an end. Part of the problem is that developing countries are being prevented from benefitting from the fruits of their wealth of natural resources[186]. This is a critical issue in the ecological emergency. Resources are being extracted from developing countries to fuel the industry and economy in developed countries. This creates a poverty trap as developing nations are often in debt to developed nations and thus can never fully reach their full potential due to this burden of debt. This reinforces the need to promote projects which contribute to the development and organisation of the economic and social life of all[187]. This can be achieved through solidarity, subsidiarity, justice, and openness. Any anthropological model needs to be in harmony with the dignity afforded to humanity by the Creator. World peace will only be achieved through building societies based on integral humanism.

The theme of world peace is developed by Pope Benedict XVI in his message in 2010 for the celebration of World Day of Peace. In his message he directly connects the cultivation peace and respect for the natural world. He describes creation as the foundation of God's creative endeavours[188]. It is essential we preserve creation for the peaceful co-existence of humanity. When we fail do so we can create 'environmental refugees' displacing communities and peoples from their rightful home. We understand humanities responsibility for the natural world in the context of God's covenant relationship with humanity and creation. There exists a covenant between human beings and the natural world not to misuse the natural goods of the earth God has given us. When we do so we threaten peace and the possibility of authentic, integral, human development. We need to

---

[186] Pope Benedict XVI, *Address of his Holiness Pope Benedict XVI to The Diplomatic Corps Accredited to the Holy See for the Traditional Exchange of New Year's Greetings*, [website], 2007, To the Diplomatic Corps accredited to the Holy See for the traditional exchange of New Year Greetings (January 8, 2007) | BENEDICT XVI (vatican.va), (accessed 31st January 2021).

[187] Ibid.

[188] Pope Benedict XVI, *Message of his Holiness Pope Benedict XVI for the Celebration of the World Day of Peace*, [website], 2010, 43rd World Day of Peace 2010, If You Want to Cultivate Peace, Protect Creation | BENEDICT XVI (vatican.va), (accessed 31st January 2021).

develop ecological awareness to understand the negative implications of our manipulation of the natural world and mankind. Pope Benedict XVI correctly identified the moral character of the ecological crisis. This extends to the economy where economic decisions have a moral consequence. We need to construct new models of development to ensure human activity never compromises the fruits of the earth. He states...

> The ecological crisis offers a historic opportunity to develop a common plan of action aimed at orientating the model of global development towards greater respect for creation and for integral human development inspired to values proper to charity in truth. I would advocate the adoption of a model of development based on the centrality of the human person, on the promotion and sharing of the common good, on responsibility on our realization of our need for a changed lifestyle and on prudence, the virtue which tells us what needs to be done today in view of what is happening tomorrow[189].

The important point is the need for a global strategy toward the ecological ills of the world and to bring about a necessary cultural renewal. The message is clear and emphatic, to cultivate peace we need to respect creation.

On Thursday 22nd of September 2011, Pope Benedict XVI addressed the German Bundestag. In his address he spoke about the positive scientific view of the natural world. The sciences may have a positivist view however because it is purely functional it is unable to bridge the gap to ethics and law. Although the positivist view is valuable it does not take into consideration all the dimensions of the human condition. When the positivist view considers itself sufficient then it diminishes our humanity[190]. He describes positivism as a concrete bunker with no windows in which we provide the atmosphere and lighting, in other words, artificial conditions. The

---

[189] Pope Benedict XVI, Message of his Holiness Pope Benedict XVI for the Celebration of the World Day of Peace, [website], 2010, 43rd World Day of Peace 2010, If You Want to Cultivate Peace, Protect Creation | BENEDICT XVI (vatican.va), (accessed 31st January 2021).

[190] Pope Benedict XVI, Visit to the Bundestag: Address of his Holiness Pope Benedict XVI, [website], 2011, Apostolic Journey to Germany: Visit to the Federal Parliament in the Reichstag Building (Berlin, 22 September 2011) | BENEDICT XVI (vatican.va), (accessed 31st January 2021).

ecological movement in Germany represents an attempt to open the windows and redefine our relationship with the natural environment. The youth are too recognising the earth has a dignity of its own with more than a functional value. It is not only matter to be manipulated into products as we choose. Greta Thunberg writes… "We cannot solve the crisis without treating it as a crisis. We need to keep fossil fuels in the ground, and we need to focus on equity"[191].

This too may be said for the ecology of man, who with his own nature, intellect, and will should not be manipulated. It is necessary for human freedom to realise with humility we did not create ourselves. Pope Benedict XVI rightly suggests that human rights are founded on the conviction there is a creator God. This conviction is the source of equality of all before the law, the recognition of the inviolability of human dignity, and the awareness of responsibility for our actions[192]. When we apply this to the environment, the realization that creation is a gift from the *Creator Spiritus* causes us to respect the goods of the earth and ensure their universal destination.

Laudato Si': On Care for Our Common Home

During his homily on the inauguration of his pontificate in 2013, Pope Francis asked his listeners to be *custos*, protectors of creation. Our responsibility to protect creation is a theme which has continued throughout his pontificate. His tenure is characterised by the call to recover an attitude of wonder and contemplation of creation. Before the publication of his letter in 2013, his first trip outside of mainland Italy was to the Lampedusa to welcome migrants fleeing from civil war and economic hardship. In 2015 he visited communities in the Philippines affected by Typhoon Yolanda. This indicated immediately that his Papacy would be about walking with

---

[191] Greta Thunberg, *No One is too Small to Make a Difference,* London, Penguin Books, 2019, p.16.

[192] Pope Benedict XVI, Visit to the Bundestag: Address of his Holiness Pope Benedict XVI, [website], 2011, Apostolic Journey to Germany: Visit to the Federal Parliament in the Reichstag Building (Berlin, 22 September 2011) | BENEDICT XVI (vatican.va), (accessed 31st January 2021).

the poor and the marginalised. He intended to influence the talks on climate change due to take place Paris the following year.

The publication of *Laudato Si'* in 2015 represents a direct intervention by Pope Francis in the climate change debate. The publication of the letter is a recognition that climate policy is no longer just a technical and scientific matter to be left to policy making politicians. Paul Haffner writes... "The scientific vision of the *cosmos* is insufficient to give us a complete picture; the vision of the faith is required as well"[193]. Part of the reason for the current crisis is because we have adopted a mechanistic and functional attitude toward nature which is devoid of any moral framework. With the publication of *Laudato Si'* in 2015, Pope Francis lays out a Catholic theology of creation, catholic practices about education and formation, the effect of ecology and the poor, and traditions compromising catholic spirituality[194]. There is both continuity and development in the letter as the encyclical builds upon previous Catholic social teaching and offers the faithful a new approach and a new way of thinking. What is new is that Pope Francis raises the level of Catholic Social teaching on the environment to an encyclical making it a part of the church's magisterium of social justice teaching. We will examine the central teaching and paradigm shifts taking place within the encyclical.

The very title of the letter, *Laudato Si': On Care for our Common Home*, immediately provides the reader with the purpose of the encyclical. It is possible to explain the title in two consecutive parts. The first, *Laudato Si' mi' Signore,* is taken from St. Francis of Assisi's *Canticle of Creatures*, and may be translated as 'Praise be to you my Lord'. The title relates the letter to the prayer of the patron of ecologists. The second part, 'On Care for Our Common Home, ushers in a paradigm shift'[195]. Pope Francis throughout his letter refers to the earth as our common home, which includes all created

---

[193] Paul Haffner, *Mystery of Creation,* Herefordshire, Gracewing, 2010, p.272.

[194] Kevin W. Irwin, *A Commentary on Laudato Si': Examining the Background, Contributions, Implementation, and Future of Pope Francis' Encyclical*, New York, Paulist Press, 2016, p. 12.

[195] Joshtrom Isaac Kureethadam, *The Ten Green Commandments of Laudato Si,* Minnesota, Liturgical Press, 1994, p. 20.

reality. The ecological crisis is affecting our home planet, the terminology here is more catholic than individualistic. Immediately we break free from environmental jargon and add an existential dimension as if we do not change our lifestyles then there could be terrible consequences for planet Earth. In his opening paragraph, the Pope compares our home to a sister with whom we share our life and a mother who opens her arms to embrace[196]. He immediately moves beyond the traditional Judeo – Christian attitude of stewardship which finds its origins in Genesis 2:15 to an attitude of kinship with creation.

Laudato Si' is divided into six chapters each with a theme. Chapter one examines the contours of the ecological crisis[197]. We are invited to "see" what is happening to our common home. In the beginning of the letter, we are given a role model for creation care, St. Francis of Assisi, who praises the Lord for all he has made. Chapter two, the Gospel of Creation, examines creation in the light of texts from the Old and New Testament, from Genesis to the gaze of Jesus. Chapter three looks at the human roots of the crisis including technology and globalisation. The letter views all of creation through the wide-angled lens of interconnectivity and examines anthropocentrism. Chapter four examines the concept of integral ecology and this will be our starting point. When we use the term 'Integral Ecology' we acknowledge the connection between environmental issues and cultural, economic, political, and social issues. The theme of integral ecology runs through *Laudato Si'* as the Pope's vision challenges modern dualisms between the sacred and secular, the objective and subjective, between spirit and matter, between anthropocentrism and biocentrism, between political and mystical, between spiritual and material, and between nature and culture[198]. This chapter invites the reader to 'judge' what is happening to the environment. Chapter five outlines the paths to

---

[196] Pope Francis, *Laudato Si': On Care for Our Common Home*, London, Catholic Truth Society, 2015, p. 7.

[197] Kevin W. Irwin, *A Commentary on Laudato Si': Examining the Background, Contributions, Implementation, and Future of Pope Francis' Encyclical*, New York, Paulist Press, 2016, p. 100.

[198] Dermot A. Lane, *Theology and Ecology in Dialogue: The Wisdom of Laudato Si'*, Dublin, Messenger Publications, 2020, p. 15-16.

dialogue, including collaboration between different disciplines, to reverse the damage to environment caused by recent human activity. The final chapter, Chapter six, outlines the changes in lifestyle that result from an awareness of our common origin, mutual belonging, and shared future. This chapter contains the 'action' part of the Popes method as we are led to personal ecological conversion and to action in our community. The binary approach of "either...or" is replaced with an inclusive approach of "both...and"[199].

Integral Ecology

We begin our examination of the message of Laudato Si' with a focus on chapter four. The most important theological insight running through the chapter, indeed the entire encyclical, is the theme of 'Integral Ecology'. First let us interpret the underlying metaphysics of this concept. 'Integral Ecology' refers to the interconnectedness of concern for the environment and love for our fellow human beings. It is a combination of natural and human ecology which respects the human and social dimensions. This concept represents a shift away from nature conservancy as both natural and human ecology are integrated[200]. We cannot be concerned about the preservation of eco-systems and be indifferent to the plight of the poor. The message of the letter is we are all connected to the natural world, the human family, and to future generations as evidenced by our common genetic code.[201] Joshtrom Kureethadam refers to this as the 'ontological glue' holding the letters main premises and arguments together[202]. The symbolism in the first chapters of the Genesis testifies to the relational nature of the Creator, the source of all being. This challenges the claim of autonomy from modern man. The reality is we are not autonomous but are part of a network bound together by the love of God. Ecosystems are a perfect

---

[199] Kevin W. Irwin, *A Commentary on Laudato Si': Examining the Background, Contributions, Implementation, and Future of Pope Francis' Encyclical*, New York, Paulist Press, 2016, p. 103.

[200] Ibid., p. 117.

[201] Pope Francis, *Laudato Si': On Care for Our Common Home*, London, Catholic Truth Society, 2015, p. 69.

[202] Joshtrom Isaac Kureethadam, *The Ten Green Commandments of Laudato Si*, Minnesota, Liturgical Press, 1994, p. 112.

example of the importance of interrelatedness for regenerative ability and to ensure sustainability. An example of this is the way in which ecosystems interact to disperse carbon dioxide, purify water, control illness and epidemics, form soil, and break down waste[203]. The interrelatedness and interdependence of ecosystems is the metaphysical and ontological basis for human communities. When we live in peace, the communitarian nature of our social life reflects the interconnectedness, balance, and diversity of all created reality. The ecological crisis is teaching us when we interfere with the balance and biodiversity of these eco-systems there are consequences for the natural ecology and human ecology.

The integral response to the environmental crisis will combine insights from various disciplines and will require a holistic understanding of the crisis. This is necessary due to the complex nature of the current crisis. We cannot not treat the environment in isolation and be blind to the truth of the interrelation between ecosystems and various spheres of social interaction. The interconnectedness of all things particularly has implications for economic models and societal structures and institutions. The present economic model, founded on the reductive epistemology of the modern technocratic paradigm, is not ensuring the common good[204]. This highlights the need for an economic ecology with a broader, more integral, and integrating vision that offers due consideration to the common destination of goods.

The health of a society's institutions is another factor in the integral response to the crisis. Environmental concerns cannot be considered in isolation of social concerns as we are part of nature, included in it, and in constant interaction with it[205]. When societal institutions function correctly, they ensure civic friendship and solidarity between citizens and the environment. Social ecology begins in the family and extends to the local, national, and

---

[203] Pope Francis, *Laudato Si': On Care for Our Common Home*, London, Catholic Truth Society, 2015, p. 70.

[204] Joshtrom Isaac Kureethadam, *The Ten Green Commandments of Laudato Si*, Minnesota, Liturgical Press, 1994, p. 116.

[205] Pope Francis, *Laudato Si': On Care for Our Common Home*, London, Catholic Truth Society, 2015, p. 69.

international communities. It is concerned with our interactions with the natural world and with fellow human beings. When the institutions which develop within each social stratum are weakened through injustice, violence, and loss of freedom this results in a low level of institutional effectiveness. The lack of well framed legislation and laws often results in ambiguity in relation to environmental issues. There is a need therefore for social institutions to be founded on the metaphysics of interdependence causing us to think of one world with a common plan for our common home.

In *Laudato Si'*, Pope Francis links the ecological crisis with the modern cultural crisis. A consumerist vision of humanity encouraged by the process of globalisation has the effect of levelling and diminishing cultures[206]. With the destruction of ecosystems, we are witnessing the disappearance of cultures and traditions which can be just as serious. Often the complexities of local problems are over-looked in favour of uniform regulations and attempts at technical interventions. Imported frameworks do not always fit into the culture of indigenous communities highlighting the need to be flexible and dynamic. It is imperative an integral approach to the preservation and promotion of the cultural heritage of local human communities, takes place within the cultural context of local people. The successful preservation of the cultural heritage of indigenous people depends on their active involvement and participation.

Cry of the Earth

Chapter One of *Laudato Si'* focuses on what is happening to our common home and creation care is a *leitmotiv* running throughout the entire document. The see-judge-act method is employed throughout the entire letter. The Pope makes an important point in the first chapter, it is not enough to simply gather information related to the environment without being inspired to action. Currently we are sleep walking into an ecological crisis thinking that if we simply re-cycle this will solve the crisis. The Earth, our common home, is unique as it is from the Earth that all life is formed, and it is the Earth

---

[206] Pope Francis, *Laudato Si': On Care for Our Common Home*, London, Catholic Truth Society, 2015, p. 72.

which sustains all life. When we examine solid scientific facts and empirical evidence, it is evident human activity has inflicted damage through the irresponsible use of the Earth's resources. This is closely related to an accelerated pace of life which the Pope refers to as 'rapidification'[207]. The speed of human activity is in direct contrast with the slow pace of biological evolution[208]. This accelerated change is not prioritised toward the common good and integral and sustainable human development. The extinction rates of species has increased as much as 1,000 times with an estimation to increase as much as 10,000 times over the next decades[209]. Human activity is having a negative effect on the eco-system and this manifests in pollution and waste, climate change, depletion of natural resources particularly water, and loss of biodiversity. These are what Pope Francis refers to as the 'cracks' in the planet[210]. Pollution, as we have examined is a modern phenomenon and a by-product of the industrial revolution and modern economic expansion[211]. It is caused by the modern throwaway culture and by transport, industrial fumes, substances contributing to the acidification of soil and water, fertilizers, insecticides, fungicides, herbicides, and agrotoxins (LS, 20)[212]. The modern technocratic paradigm is incapable of seeing the interconnectedness and mysterious network of relations in natural ecosystems. What is required is a circular model of production to preserve resources for present and future generations and limit the use of non-renewable resources (LS, 22)[213].

---

[207] Pope Francis, *Laudato Si': On Care for Our Common Home*, London, Catholic Truth Society, 2015, p. 15.

[208] Ibid.

[209] Joshtrom Isaac Kureethadam, *The Ten Green Commandments of Laudato Si*, Minnesota, Liturgical Press, 1994, p. 27.

[210] Pope Francis, *Laudato Si': On Care for Our Common Home*, London, Catholic Truth Society, 2015, p. 80.

[211] Joshtrom Isaac Kureethadam, *The Ten Green Commandments of Laudato Si*, Minnesota, Liturgical Press, 1994, p. 27.

[212] Pope Francis, *Laudato Si': On Care for Our Common Home*, London, Catholic Truth Society, 2015, p. 16.

[213] Ibid., p. 17.

Next the letter focuses on climate, described by Pope Francis as a 'common good' (*LS*, 23)[214]. The climate is a vital source of life for every living creature. The root cause of global warming is a model of development based on the intensive use of fossil fuels and increased change is uses of soil (*LS*, 23)[215]. The concentration of greenhouse gases emitted into the earth's atmosphere is a result of human activity in the last decades. The knock-on effects of this include an increase in extreme weather events, a constant rise in sea level, pressure on availability of essential resources like water, extinction of the planet's biodiversity, melting of polar ice caps in high altitude plains, the loss of tropical forests, and the acidification of the oceans. Pope Francis warns if we continue with our current lifestyles it will lead to unprecedented climate change and long-term destruction of important eco-systems. The prevailing technocratic paradigm is convincing societies the Earth's resources are infinite justifying the alarming rate of extraction. Of course, this is untrue, and the current rate of extraction is unsustainable. If we continue at this rate it will have negative consequences for future generations. The same may be said of the loss of biodiversity due to human activity, as year after year thousands of plant and animal species disappear. Biodiversity is essential for human needs like nutrition, medicine and regulating ecosystems. For this reason, plant and animal species have an intrinsic value in themselves[216]. Due to the interrelatedness of living creatures, all species play a critical role in maintaining the balance and equilibrium of eco-systems. The main point of the letter here is that there are several interlinked physical crises destroying our common home.

The human environment is equally affected by environmental deterioration. There are many social dimensions of global climate change including loss of employment due to technological innovations, social exclusion, inequitable distribution and consumption of energy, social break down, increased violence, and a

---

[214] Pope Francis, *Laudato Si': On Care for Our Common Home*, London, Catholic Truth Society, 2015, p. 17.

[215] Ibid.

[216] Joshtrom Isaac Kureethadam, *The Ten Green Commandments of Laudato Si*, Minnesota, Liturgical Press, 1994, p. 31.

rise in new forms of social aggression such as drug trafficking, increased drug use by young people, and loss of identity (*LS*, 46)[217]. Technological advances, although affording exciting possibilities, have caused a type of mental pollution and reduced the opportunity for genuine encounter. Human and social degradation are closely connected with environmental degradation. Both are interrelated and often the most vulnerable are most affected. Pope Francis righty points out that any ecological approach will always be a social approach.

Cry of the Poor

As we have already stated the poor are disproportionately affected by the climate crisis. It is for this reason an authentic ecological approach will need to have a social dimension. It will only be successful if it respects the dignity of the poor and displays solidarity with the most vulnerable in communities. To be successful in any endeavour it is imperative that we listen not only the cry of the earth but also to the cry of the poor. Pope Francis refers to the preferential option of the poor as an 'ethical imperative' (*LS*, 158)[218]. *Laudato Si'* is fundamentally a letter on social justice and not specifically climate change. This is evidenced by the fact climate is mentioned fourteen times, the poor fifty-nine times, and creation sixty-six times[219]. He identifies one area in need of revision is the living conditions within our metropolis which have become unhealthy due to pollution. It is the poor living in dehumanizing urban landscapes that suffer the most in these habitats.

The poor make up the majority of the world's population, yet they use the least of the Earth's resources. They suffer the most from climate change and contribute the least to global warming. Often the poor are those who are forced to migrate from their homeland due to

---

[217] Pope Francis, *Laudato Si': On Care for Our Common Home*, London, Catholic Truth Society, 2015, p. 25.

[218] Ibid., p. 76.

[219] Joshtrom Isaac Kureethadam, *The Ten Green Commandments of Laudato Si*, Minnesota, Liturgical Press, 1994, p. 37.

poverty caused by environmental degradation (*LS* 25)[220]. These issues, and the quality of water in poor countries, are some of the symptoms of the moral travesty of the climate crisis. The disproportionate effects of the crisis are most evident in indigenous communities. Often, they are forced from their homelands to facilitate the projects of multinational companies. This has devastating effects on the environment as the aim of agricultural and mining projects is to make profit and not to preserve the ecosystem and culture of those who are displaced. It is essential indigenous communities are the principal dialogue partners when large projects effecting their land are proposed. For them, the land is not a commodity but a sacred place to express their culture and traditions (*LS* 146)[221]. The reality is that indigenous peoples know best how to care for their land.

Laudato Si' makes a direct connection between social and ecological justice. It is only when we integrate questions of justice in debates on the environment that we begin to hear both the cry of the earth and the cry of the poor[222]. Both are inextricably linked as it is the same thinking which leaves no room for sincere concern for the environment which lacks concern for the inclusion of vulnerable members of human societies (*LS* 196)[223]. The reason the crisis is related to justice is because the environmental degradation is caused by the rich minority and it is the innocent poor and vulnerable who are most affected. One of the biggest millstones around the necks of the poor is what is known as 'ecological debt'. One possible measure of this debt is the ecological footprint of nations and individuals as this is an indicator of human pressure on the physical world. It may be calculated using humanities consumption of natural resources, use of ecological services, and production of pollution and waste[224]. The ecological debt exists mostly between the global north and south and

---

[220] Pope Francis, *Laudato Si': On Care for Our Common Home*, London, Catholic Truth Society, 2015, p. 18.

[221] Ibid., p. 73.

[222] Ibid., p. 27.

[223] Ibid., p. 94.

[224] Joshtrom Isaac Kureethadam, *The Ten Green Commandments of Laudato Si*, Minnesota, Liturgical Press, 1994, p. 44.

is mainly caused by commercial imbalances and disproportionate use of natural resources over long periods of time. The over extraction of natural resources by the global north has cause a depletion of these resources in the global south. This causes developing countries to have their development potential diminished through lack of resources and crippling debt. One possible solution to this is to encourage responsibility for our carbon footprint in the west at a personal level by communities, households, and individuals. This will help to create parity in the consumption of natural resources across the globe and eliminate the ecological apartheid which presently exists.

As the title of the letter suggest the Earth is our common home therefore, we have a common responsibility to care for the Earth. As the negative consequences of the climate crisis are differentiated so too is responsibility differentiated (*LS* 52). This point is made by the United States Bishops when they state that we need to listen to the needs of the poor, the weak and the vulnerable in a debate dominated by the interests of the powerful[225]. The concept of common and differentiated responsibilities will ensure those countries that have caused the most damage to the environment will have the greater responsibility to provide a solution to the problems they have caused.

When we believe that we are members of one single human family, living in our common household the Earth and its atmosphere, then each person has equal rights to the Earth's resources and atmosphere. The climate is a common good and when we deny this to any member of our human family then this becomes an issue of ecological and social justice. For Pope Francis, due to the concept of differentiated responsibilities, we always need to display the preferential option of the poor in the climate debate. His letter is in effect a summons to solidarity with the poor. The moral and ethical dimension of the debate is most evident when we examine the ecological crisis in the context of ecological justice. Each member of the human family has the responsibility to make the world more equitable for each member of the human family. The current

---

[225] United States Conference of Catholic Bishops, Global Climate Change A Plea for Dialogue Prudence and the Common Good, [website], 2001, Global Climate Change A Plea for Dialogue Prudence and the Common Good | USCCB, (accessed 10th February 2021).

ecological crisis has indicated the importance of listening to the voice of the poor. We have a moral and ethical responsibility to focus on their needs in a debate where the interests of the powerful have dominated. When we examine the current ecological crisis in the context of our common future then this helps us to prioritise the needs of the poor to ensure the common good for all members of our human family. This will be the only sustainable solution to the current crisis. There is also the urgent need for action however this action will only be possible within a framework of social and ecological justice.

The five principles of Catholic Social teaching, outlined by the American Bishops in a document about Global Climate Change in 2001, serve as a guideline in our attitude towards the poor. First there is the need to work towards the universal common good. Secondly all members of our common household have the right to equity, economic initiative and be stewards of creation. The third is authentic development will acknowledge the impact of consumerism and is concerned with protecting the dignity of each person behind every demographic considering their cultural norms, faith, and moral values[226]. The fourth is caring for the poor and issues of equity and the fifth is the public policy debate and future directions. These five points constitute the 'action' part of the Pope Francis' "see-judge-act" methodology in *Laudato Si'*. If, after identifying these issues, we fail to act then we are inadvertently worsening the suffering of the most vulnerable members of our human family. Listening to the cry of the poor challenges our lifestyles in developed countries causing us to rethink current models of production and consumption, models which support and lead us to a culture of relativism. Rethinking our current models hopefully will lead us to ecological conversion and more sober lifestyles ensuring we take only our fair share of the Earth's resources.

Cry of the Children

The notion of the common good extends to future generations. The most effective decisions in the climate debate will express

---

[226] Kevin W. Irwin, *A Commentary on Laudato Si': Examining the Background Contributions*, Implementation, and Future of Pope Francis's Encyclical, New York, Paulist Press, 2016, p.54 – 55.

intergenerational solidarity. This concept will be essential for development to be authentic and sustainable. Our present rate of consumption of the Earth's resources displays a blatant disregard for the next generation. Pope Francis warns in his letter that future generations will disproportionately incur the costs of current ecological degradation[227]. The current crisis challenges us to think about our world view and about the world the next generation will inherit from us[228]. It is a direct challenge to the utilitarian world view which promotes a culture of individualism and relativism. When we believe the world is a gift from God this includes the responsibility to preserve the gift for future generations. We need to ensure future generations are not inheriting a world to which we have inflicted irreversible damage.

Laudato Si' clarifies the notion of intergenerational solidarity is not simply related to ecological policy making, it is closely related to the obligation of justice. The Portuguese Bishops expressed this sentiment when they stated…

> The environment lies in the logic of reception: it is a loan that each generation receives and must transmit to the next generation. Hence the enormous responsibility for the use and enjoyment of common environmental goods in each historical present. Future generations have the right to receive the environment in better conditions than the situations in which previous generations have lived it[229].

Our responsibility to future generations includes struggling with current ecological issues for the sake of our own dignity. Ultimately this will lead us to the deeper existential questions as we grapple with the purpose of life's pilgrimage here on Earth. Our starting point needs to be a critical examination of the current pace of consumption which stretches the capacity of the planet's finite resources. This calls for decisive action here and now to replace the

---

[227] Pope Francis, *Laudato Si': On Care for Our Common Home*, London, Catholic Truth Society, 2015, p. 78.

[228] *Tata Pravesh #Doorway to Green*, [Online Video], 2018, Tata Pravesh | #DoorwayToGreen - YouTube, (accessed 5th April 2021).

[229] Portuguese Bishops, *Portuguese Episcopal Conference: Joint responsibility for the common good*, [website], 2003, Responsabilidade solidária pelo bem comum - Conferência Episcopal Portuguesa (conferenciaepiscopal.pt), (accessed 9th March 2033).

existing technocratic paradigm which encourages rampant individualism and a self-centred culture of instant gratification[230]. The first place of ecological conversion will be the home and family where we learn the importance of intergenerational solidarity.

One child constantly reminding us of the urgency of the climate emergency is Greta Thunberg. In May 2018 Greta was a winner in a writing competition about the environment held by *Svenska Dagbladet*, a Swedish newspaper. On the August 20th, Greta went on a school- strike outside the Swedish parliament building to highlight the climate crisis, handing out flyers listing facts about the climate crisis and explanations. Her posts on Instagram and Twitter documenting the reasons for her action went viral. When we read about the 'Cry of the Children' in *Laudato Si'* immediately Greta springs to mind as she is constantly reminding us of how decision-makers are sacrificing civilisation for the opportunity of a small number of people to make enormous amounts of money[231]. Our youth are challenging companies into climate action because they realize the future of our living planet is at stake. Our current lifestyles have placed eco-systems at tipping point and if we continue it will cause a chain reaction that will affect our survival as a civilization. Rock-solid science is teaching us this. Greta represents what can be achieved through action and conviction.

Ecological Conversion: Personal and Communal Response

What we see in the light of the most recent papal teaching should cause us to judge and inspire us to act. The last three chapters of *Laudato Si'* are dedicated to what our response to the ecological crisis should be. The first response, a common thread running through the letter, is to develop an integral ecology and a holistic approach to the crisis. This demands a new vision and the recognition of the interrelatedness and interconnectedness of the human and social dimensions. The interrelatedness of things is an essential part

---

[230] Pope Francis, *Laudato Si': On Care for Our Common Home*, London, Catholic Truth Society, 2015, p. 79.

[231] Greta Thunberg, *No One is too Small to Make a Difference*, London, Penguin Books, 2019, p. 18.

of the divine plan as our interdependence reflects our incompleteness. Often humanity has justified their dominion over the Earth by claiming autonomy. This is of course untrue as the law of life on the planet is governed by relatedness of one creature to another. Ecosystems, for example, function only because of an intricate network of species within the eco-system. We have learned over time that the slightest interference in an ecosystem can have fatal consequences. An integral approach to the crisis will consider the contribution from various disciplines.

Human beings are themselves made from the dust of the Earth (Gen 2:7). We are also made *Imago Dei* (Gen 1:26). Because we are made in God's image, we have a unique place in the world and in our relationship with our surroundings (*LS* 15)[232]. Because of our uniqueness a renewal of our relationship with nature will necessitate a renewal of human ecology. Human ecology refers not only to the environments where we live, which reflect our identity, but also the relationship between human life and the moral law written on our hearts[233]. The ecology of man begins with the acceptance of our bodies and the way we interact with the natural world and members of the human family. When we accept our bodies as a gift from the creator, we are better able to live in harmony with our surroundings and find mutual enrichment with other members of the human family. The reverse is also true, when we see ourselves as autonomous enjoying absolute power over or bodies, this can lead us to think we enjoy absolute power over creation. Integral humanism is therefore an essential ingredient in creating an integral ecology. We may draw lessons from the story of Cain and Able in the scriptures (Genesis 4: 9-11). We each have the responsibility to care for our neighbour. When we do this justice will dwell in the land and life will be preserved. Therefore, a Catholic theology of creation is an integral

---

[232] Pope Francis, *Laudato Si': On Care for Our Common Home*, London, Catholic Truth Society, 2015, p.13.

[233] Ibid., p.76.

theology which acknowledges the communal relatedness of the Earth, all creatures, and each member of the human family to God[234].

Ecology may only be considered integral when we incorporate the social dimension. When we use the word 'environment' we are referring to the relationship between nature and society (*LS* 139)[235]. We are in constant interaction with the environment and environmental issues are related to social issues such as the social organization of human communities and the health of our institutions. Pope Francis reminds us in the letter there is not one environmental crisis and social crisis but one complex social and environmental crisis (*LS* 139)[236]. We cannot therefore separate our concern for the environment from our concern for the plight of our fellow human beings. This is the important social dimension of the crisis as outlined on the letter. As with the story of Cain and Able when we declare autonomy, social structures being to collapse.

Laudato Si' provides the reader with clear guidelines of how to live in our common home locally, nationally and internationally. It also identifies the root cause of the crisis which is human i.e., the current social and economic systems. What we need is a new economic and political ecology because the existing paradigms are built on a myth of infinite growth. A new approach will bring about both the reduction of poverty and the reduction of pollution. The new economy needs to make provision for the poor and respect the natural cycle of eco-systems. We cannot have one plan for the rich developed countries and one plan for the poor developing countries due to our interdependence. We need to be more inclusive with our dialogue and decide to create one common plan (*LS* 164)[237]. The international community will be instrumental in implementing our way forward. Conventions such as the Basil Convention on hazardous waste, and agreements such as the Paris Climate Agreement in 2016 have been

---

[234] Kevin W. Irwin, *A Commentary on Laudato Si': Examining the Background Contributions*, Implementation, and Future of Pope Francis's Encyclical, New York, Paulist Press, 2016, p.174.

[235] Pope Francis, *Laudato Si': On Care for Our Common Home*, London, Catholic Truth Society, 2015, p.69.

[236] Ibid., p.124.

[237] Ibid., p.128.

successful in providing targets for countries to achieve within a given timeframe. However, their success will be dependent upon consensus by all nations on the guidelines and observance of the limitations set in the agreements. Another vital element will be the recognition of common and differentiated responsibilities due to the fact countries with scarce resources will require assistance for many years in the future (*LS* 170)[238]. Developed countries also have the responsibility to display solidarity with developing nations helping them to access the technology and financial resources they need to reach their full potential. There is enormous potential for international agreement and collaboration in relation to what Pope Francis refers to as the 'global commons' such as the Oceans (*LS* 174)[239]. There is also the need to set long- term goals.

To manage our common home effectively, Pope Francis indicated in his letter, there is the need for the new way of doing economics. We can no longer think about economics simply in terms of profit. We need a new interpretation of economics, moving towards something like *the* German concept of *Wirtschaft.* This means handling or taking care of our common household, as the Greeks would say, *oikos + nomos,* which means the law or the rule of one's household[240]. Existing economic models have cause immeasurable damage to our surroundings as they see the Earth's resources purely for human consumption. This is a misunderstanding of the concept of economics, when increased production becomes the only goal with little thought to the desertification of the land, loss of biodiversity and the increase in pollution. Businesses rarely incur the costs of the pollution created because of production and this creates a moral and ethical dilemma. These costs are both economic and social. The reality is the current market economy is inadequate in ensuring integral human development for each member of the human

---

[238] Pope Francis, *Laudato Si': On Care for Our Common Home*, London, Catholic Truth Society, 2015, p.129.

[239] Ibid., p.84.

[240] Kevin W. Irwin, *A Commentary on Laudato Si': Examining the Background Contributions*, Implementation, and Future of Pope Francis's Encyclical, New York, Paulist Press, 2016, p.131 – 132.

family and creates an economy of exclusion and inequality[241]. Ecological economics challenges the economics of exclusion. It will also challenge societies to redefine their concepts of development and progress. Ideally, we seek to achieve the circular model of production, as exemplified by the natural eco-systems when they replenish their by-products. This is the only way we can preserve resources for future generations. Immediately we need to diversify from the use of fossil fuels to create energy. This will necessitate creativity and financing from government agencies as we transition to cleaner, alternative forms of energy. Our planetary and economic systems need to be harmonious. A new economic model will only be successful within a political framework supporting its aims and objectives.

A new political culture will also be essential to manage our common home effectively. Many existing policies related to the environment are outdated and no longer applicable to the present situation. Current environmental polices need to be rethought and rewritten to include far sighted environmental goals and to limit a culture of short-term gain and private interest. Today's politics is often influenced by unjust economic models with little or no regard for the common good. The Pope states categorically Politics must not be subject to the economy just as the economy should not be subject to the efficiency driven paradigm of technocracy[242]. Both politics and the economy need to be reorientated toward the common good. Market forces prioritize profits and are unconcerned about the rhythms of nature and biodiversity. We need to create a new political culture capable of an integral and interdisciplinary approach to the climate crisis. This is necessary because it will not be possible to write effective environmental policies and rethink existing processes when politics is subservient to economics. *Laudato Si'* renews the appeal of Pope John Paul II and Pope Benedict XVI in calling for the creation of a global institution to manage the current crisis, the global

---

[241] Pope Francis, *Evangelii Gaudium*, [website], 2013, Evangelii Gaudium : Apostolic Exhortation on the Proclamation of the Gospel in Today's World (24 November 2013) | Francis (vatican.va), (accessed 14th February 2021).

[242] Pope Francis, *Laudato Si': On Care for Our Common Home*, London, Catholic Truth Society, 2015, p.90.

economy, and to establish long term goals and prioritize the common good.

From a social perspective, the climate crisis is redefining our concept of citizenship. It is evident there is an urgent need for our concept of citizenship to include an ecological dimension. An awareness of our common origin, acknowledgement that the Earth is our common home, and the realization we have a shared future all provide the inspiration to redefine our lifestyles. One way to bring about the change in lifestyle will be through education. Chapter six of *Laudato Si'* is dedicated to the cultural, spiritual and educational challenge to develop new convictions, attitudes and forms of life (*LS* 202)[243]. Joshtrom Kureethadam refers to ecological education and spirituality as two wings which can enable a person to take off on the lifelong journey of ecological conversion. One of the reasons for the necessity of spiritual renewal and ecological conversion is due to the deep moral root of the crisis. Pope Francis writes…

> The current global situation engenders a feeling of instability and uncertainty, which in turn becomes "a seedbed for collective selfishness". When people become self-centred and self-enclosed, their greed increases. The emptier a person's heart is the more he or she needs things to buy, own and consume. It becomes almost impossible to accept the limits imposed by reality[244].

The aim of the letter is to encourage an ecological conversion that will ultimately cause us to change consumption driven lifestyles. Laudato Si' supports the re-establishment of a covenant relationship between humanity and creation. Environmental education needs to be holistic and seek to restore harmony between humanity, nature and the divine. The radical change required to live sustainable lifestyles requires us to be countercultural. One sure way to be countercultural is to choose a lifestyle with goals independent of technology. Another way will be to choose a lifestyle which is not driven by compulsive consumerism and leads to genuine freedom. Education, especially for the youth, will be an important vehicle in bringing about the change

---

[243] Pope Francis, *Laudato Si': On Care for Our Common Home*, London, Catholic Truth Society, 2015, p.97.

[244] Ibid., p.98.

in lifestyle. Education will help to instil important values and create responsible stewards as is evident in the number of young people who are displaying ecological sensitivity (*LS* 209)[245]. The utilitarian mindset advocating individualism, unlimited progress, competition, and consumerism, is slowly being replaced with restoration of the ecological equilibrium, and the establishment of harmony within ourselves, with other human beings, with the natural world and with God (*LS* 210)[246]. The existing system of education, founded upon anthropocentrism and autonomy, favours a mechanistic vision of the natural world. The curricula in modern education systems portray the Earth as a source of unlimited natural resources. It seeks to prepare students to be competitive in global markets and measure their success in terms of economic profit. *Laudato Si'* advocates revising curricula to include integral humanism and integral ecology which will help to resist the technocratic paradigm. A more holistic education will harmonise our relationships with the natural world, with fellow human beings, and with the divine creator. The revised curricula will prepare students for long term sustainability rather than short term profit. This will create citizens who are responsible stewards of the environment rather than autonomous individuals with a mechanistic view of nature. A holistic education will challenge the existing mindset and increase solidarity within the human family and prioritise the common good. It will also bring about the changes in lifestyle which will be vital for the future of our common household. Ecological education will have theology at its centre and not anthropology. In fact, a successful measure of the effectiveness of education will be its ability to instil a deep sense of our dependence on the creator for our existence and the existence of all things on the universe. Students should be filled with wonder and awe when contemplating creation appreciating its integrity and beauty beyond utility and consumption[247].

---

[245] Pope Francis, *Laudato Si': On Care for Our Common Home*, London, Catholic Truth Society, 2015, p.99.

[246] Ibid., p.100.

[247] Joshtrom Isaac Kureethadam, *The Ten Green Commandments of Laudato Si*, Minnesota, Liturgical Press, 1994, p. 153.

There are a variety of settings for ecological education beginning with the family, school and within societies. Political institutions, social groups like the Global Catholic Climate Movement, and the Church all have a role to play in creating responsible stewards and more sustainable lifestyles. Possibly the first place we learn integral ecology is the family where we are taught self-control and respect for our surroundings (*LS* 213)[248]. The responsibility for ecological education should not belong to our schools, but political institution also have a role to play in raising awareness. Political Institutions also need the ability to enforce penalties when individuals and corporations exceed the agreed limits for sustainability.

The end goal of ecological education is ecological conversion and the development of an authentic creation spirituality[249]. Our response will be multi-dimensional involving both an interior conversion and repentance for the sins committed against God and God's gift of creation. An ecological conversion will motivate and inspire us to gestures of care towards our common home and the members of our common household. An individual response will not be enough to solve the complex social problems caused by the ecological crisis. The task of caring for our common home will need to involve community networks and employ the skills from various disciplines to bring about a community conversion (*LS* 219)[250]. When we approach creation care with a spirit of repentance then the exercise becomes less about recycling, down-sizing, and resource management and more about returning to God and re-establishing harmony and equilibrium with the source of the theophany we call nature. When we, as individuals and as a community, repent for the damage we have caused to the environment then God will forgive and heal the Earth (2 Chr. 7:17). We first need to reorientate ourselves toward the creator of all things. The second step in our ecological conversion will be turning back to nature itself and serving

---

[248] Pope Francis, *Laudato Si': On Care for Our Common Home*, London, Catholic Truth Society, 2015, p.101.

[249] Joshtrom Isaac Kureethadam, *The Ten Green Commandments of Laudato Si,* Minnesota, Liturgical Press, 1994, p. 161.

[250] Pope Francis, *Laudato Si': On Care for Our Common Home*, London, Catholic Truth Society, 2015, p.104.

the Earth (Gen. 3:19). This is a return to our original vocation to till and keep the garden (Gen. 2:15). Our conversion will include fostering attitudes of generous and tender care which is possible when we understand creation as a loving gift from the Father. It is for his exemplary attitude to the development of the fraternity of creation that St. Francis of Assisi is a model for ecological conversion and creation spirituality. St. Francis provides us with the radical 'Kinship Model' of creation inspiring the faithful to think big and act small as love for creation and other members of our common household find expression in small caring gestures. This helps to develop a culture of care.

Ecology and Liturgy: Celebrating the Cosmic Eucharist

Christianity's vision of creation, the earth, and its resources is sacramental and thus finds God in all things. A leaf, a dewdrop, a mountain trail, a poor person's face may have a mystical meaning (*LS* 233)[251]. In Christian spirituality all the natural world speaks to us of the presence of God and offers an occasion for divine encounter. This concept is supported in the writings of St. Bonaventure and St. Augustine. Bonaventure sees the universe as a wonderful work of art and one can see in the universe traces of the maker in the way one sees traces of an artist in a painting. The book of revelation is a metaphor St. Augustine used to describe nature and when we read it correctly it leads us to God. Created realities are a means of communion with the divine and this finds perfection in the Christian theology and praxis of the sacraments. *Laudato Si'* highlights the way in which the sacramental life of the Church takes up natural elements such as water, fire and oil, and incorporates them into acts of ritual. The Sacraments transform the fruits of the Earth to become a means of communion with God. The archetype of all sacramental activity is when Christ became man at the Incarnation. The *Logos* becoming flesh represents the intimate meeting and inextricable intertwining of

---

[251] Pope Francis, *Laudato Si': On Care for Our Common Home*, London, Catholic Truth Society, 2015, p.109.

both the spiritual and the material[252]. The sacramental world view is personified in the person of Christ as creation becomes a medium of divine revelation. This is what sets Christianity apart from other systems of belief because it does not reject matter rather it embraces the inner nature of the human body as a temple of the Holy Spirit (*LS* 235)[253]. Incarnational spirituality reaches its summit in the celebration of the Eucharist for it is in this sacrament that grace is tangibly manifested when God gave himself as food for his creatures (*LS* 236)[254]. In *Laudato Si'*, the celebration of the Eucharist is fundamental to our understanding of the cosmos and describes the sacrament as 'an act of cosmic love' (*LS* 236)[255]. The reason for this is through the fragmentation of matter God reaches our intimate depths by joining heaven and earth. It at one and the same time both penetrates and embraces all of creation. When the Eucharist is celebrated creation is projected toward divinization[256].

Scholars such as Dermot A. Lane have studied the mutual interaction between Ecology and Liturgy to understand better their role in a response to the climate emergency. According to Dermot A. Lane there is not much reference to creation in the Liturgy of the Eucharist which means our liturgical prayers are schizophrenic[257]. This statement from Lane requires clarification. He is pointing to the tragedy of believing in one thing and celebrating something different. The Liturgy could be a vehicle for inspiring worshipping communities to ecological conversion. The Liturgy may also provide a sacred space for recognition of the sinfulness of ecological degradation and for restoring the integrity of creation through reconciliation. Ecology may also help the liturgy to establish a connection between the Eucharist and the natural world. This will allow us to reconnect to the original sources of the Liturgy: creation,

---

[252] Joshtrom Isaac Kureethadam, *The Ten Green Commandments of Laudato Si*, Minnesota, Liturgical Press, 1994, p. 174.

[253] Pope Francis, *Laudato Si': On Care for Our Common Home*, London, Catholic Truth Society, 2015, p.110.

[254] Ibid.

[255] Ibid.

[256] Ibid.

[257] Dermot A. Lane, *Theology and Ecology in Dialogue: The Wisdom of Laudato Si'*, Dublin, Messenger Publications, 2020, p. 9.

the Last Passover, the institution of the Eucharist, the work of social and ecological justice, and the connection between creation and eschatology[258].

The modern era has contributed to increasing the distance between the liturgy and creation. In the Jewish tradition there is a strong sense of the close connection between creation and the liturgy. For example, there are seven accounts of creation in the Old Testament. The authorship of Genesis chapter one by Priests in the Jewish Temple (6th Century BCE) indicates the purpose and intention have to do with liturgy and worship. The structure of the Genesis account of creation indicates liturgical usage. The theme of the goodness of creation is continued in the Psalms. The Psalms implicitly link creation and worship as we are inspired by the wonder of creation to bow down (Psalm 95). The prophet Isaiah describes nature as the throne of God (Isaiah 66: 1-2). The Old Testament scriptures also give us a sense of the imminent presence of God in the world. The created world is sacramental in nature and a place of encounter with the divine. For our ancestors, creation was a sacred place which inspired wonder and awe and invited worship and praise. The mechanisation of nature and our modern lifestyles have caused us to lose our sense of enchantment when we contemplate the universe. We have reduced creation to an object to be exploited. Dermot A. Lane writes… "With this mechanization of nature, the earth lost its voice. Talk about nature was taken over by the language of science, the free market and economic efficiency"[259]. The integrity of nature was replaced in social consciousness with the desire to manage and dominate the natural world. There is no doubt this is partly due to modern theologies of creation characterised by the dominion model. The anthropocentric nature of the stewardship model of creation, portraying humans as independent, external, and separate from the rest of creation, also causes problems for the theocentric nature of liturgy and worship. The 'Community model of

---

[258] Dermot A. Lane, *Theology and Ecology in Dialogue: The Wisdom of Laudato Si'*, Dublin, Messenger Publications, 2020, p. 115.

[259] Ibid., p. 116.

Creation' is the only model to open up possibilities for the Liturgy[260]. When the relationship between humanity and the rest of creation becomes one of kinship, then the liturgy becomes the universe giving praise to God. *Laudato Si'* states we are a part of nature, included in it and in constant interaction with it (*LS* 139)[261]. Through the community of creation model, we rediscover our interdependence and interrelatedness with the natural world. By doing this we extend our concept of neighbour beyond fellow humans to the natural world. As liturgies are communal events, all of creation is included in our worship of God. When our concept of liturgy shifts to include the whole of creation giving praise to God then the attitude of domination changes to one of kinship, the act of exploiting becomes respect, and competition becomes cooperation[262]. God's incarnation in the person of Christ and his passion, death and resurrection is for the entire *cosmos*. Nature is often the subject of the parabolic teaching of Jesus as its diversity, cycles and rhythms are indicative of the harmony in God's kingdom. The community of creation model is intrinsic to our understanding of the 'Cosmic Eucharist'. When we read the book of nature, we are humbled by the sense of 'sublime communion' existing within (*LS* 89)[263]. It is symbolic and sacramental in character (*LS* 9)[264]. Natural elements are intrinsic in the sacraments to mediate the supernatural life (*LS* 235). The concept of the participation of the cosmic liturgy in the Christological drama is proving inaccessible to modern Christians due to the process of urbanisation[265]. The Eucharist is one sacrament where the natural elements are raised to the level the level of theology.

---

[260] Dermot A. Lane, *Theology and Ecology in Dialogue: The Wisdom of Laudato Si'*, Dublin, Messenger Publications, 2020, p. 131.

[261] Pope Francis, *Laudato Si': On Care for Our Common Home*, London, Catholic Truth Society, 2015, p. 69.

[262] Dermot A. Lane, *Theology and Ecology in Dialogue: The Wisdom of Laudato Si'*, Dublin, Messenger Publications, 2020, p. 132.

[263] Pope Francis, *Laudato Si': On Care for Our Common Home*, London, Catholic Truth Society, 2015, p. 46.

[264] Ibid., p. 10.

[265] Dermot A. Lane, *Theology and Ecology in Dialogue: The Wisdom of Laudato Si'*, Dublin, Messenger Publications, 2020, p. 139.

Dermott A Lane divides the statements on the Eucharist in *Laudato Si'* into a number of categories Theocentric dimensions, Christocentric dimensions, Creation-centred dimensions, Cosmocentric dimensions, and Eco-centric dimensions[266]. Each dimension prompts further liturgical and theological reflection on the Eucharist. The Cosmo-centric dimension teaches the Eucharist is an act of cosmic love where the whole cosmos gives thanks to God (*LS* 236). Even when celebrated on the altar of a country church it is celebrated on the altar of the world (LS 236). Each dimension rediscovers the biblical link, lost by modern man, between the Eucharist and creation. The Eucharist also points to the eschatological character of the cosmos when God will be all in all[267]. This is part of the vision of Teilhard de Chardin when in the end we will have a true cosmic liturgy, where the cosmos will become a living host[268]. The Eucharist also has a penitential aspect and may be the source of healing for our broken relationships with God, the human family, and the earth.

Pope Francis in *Laudato Si'* endorses liturgical renewal based on the *cosmic* character of the Eucharist[269]. The Eucharist has the power to cause a shift in the way humans see themselves within a universal context and to be a source of ecological and social justice. Teilhard de Chardin re-establishes the link between the Eucharist and the *cosmos*. His vision highlights how cosmology can deepen our understanding and celebration of the Eucharist as Christ descends into the Host of the world. The cycle of life death and rebirth in the *cosmos is* evident in the Christological drama of the Eucharist. The breaking of the bread and the pouring of the wine is the sacramental representation of the life death and resurrection of *Jesus*. The ingredients of the Eucharist, made from the raw elements of the Earth, are transformed through the incantations of the priest and the creative action of the Spirit into the Body and Blood of Christ. The

---

[266] Dermot A. Lane, *Theology and Ecology in Dialogue: The Wisdom of Laudato Si'*, Dublin, Messenger Publications, 2020, p. 40.

[267] Ibid., p. 141.

[268] Pope Benedict XVI, *Celebration of Vespers with the Faithful of Aosta: Homily of his Holiness Benedict XVI*, [website], 2009, 24 July 2009: Celebration of Vespers in the Cathedral of Aosta | BENEDICT XVI (vatican.va)(accessed 21st February 2021).

[269] Dermot A. Lane, *Theology and Ecology in Dialogue: The Wisdom of Laudato Si'*, Dublin, Messenger Publications, 2020, p. 143.

Eucharist is an act of cosmic worship because it brings the whole universe to the altar in an act of thanksgiving and love[270]. The celebration of the Eucharist on a Sunday connects our worship with the Jewish Sabbath and the day of *Jesus'* resurrection. This reminds us of God's contemplative rest in Genesis 2: 1-3 after his act of creation and the first day of the new creation when Christ is risen from the dead[271].

The Trinitarian dimension of Creation Spirituality

The Trinity is the revelation of God as Father, Son and Holy Spirit and the subsequent subsistent relations between each person of the Trinity. The relationality of everything in the universe, according to Christianity, is evidence of the mark of the Trinity. St. Thomas Aquinas developed a Trinitarian idea of creation. He systematically presents the Trinitarian principles acing within creation and repercussions for our understanding of the created world[272]. An ascending model of the Trinity, the point of departure for the community model of creation, highlights the action of the Spirit throughout the whole of creation. The interconnectedness, relatedness and interdependence is grounded in a Spirit driven theology of creation[273]. When we believe humanity to be made *Imago Dei* then the relational anthropology between the Father, Son and Holy Spirit will resonate with our experience of being human. For example, according to Saint Augustine the image of the Trinity is to be found in the intellectual nature of the soul and its three powers, the Memory (the Father), Intellect (the Son), and the Will (the Holy Ghost). *Laudato Si'* describes the Father as the ultimate source of all things, the Son is united to the earth in becoming man and the Spirit

---

[270] Joshtrom Isaac Kureethadam, *The Ten Green Commandments of Laudato Si,* Minnesota, Liturgical Press, 1994, p. 176.

[271] Pope Francis, *Laudato Si': On Care for Our Common Home*, London, Catholic Truth Society, 2015, p. 111.

[272] Gilles Emery, *The Trinitarian Theology of St. Thomas Aquinas*, Oxford, Oxford University Press, 2007, p. 338.

[273] Dermot A. Lane, *Theology and Ecology in Dialogue: The Wisdom of Laudato Si',* Dublin, Messenger Publications, 2020, p. 126.

is at the heart of the universe inspiring and renewing (*LS* 238)[274]. In *Laudato Si'* the three persons in the Trinity are present in all of creation and has left its mark in all of creation. St. Francis taught that every creature reflects the Trinitarian nature of God except we cannot always see this because our gaze is darkened due to the fall.

The web of relations in the universe is based on the divine model and therefore reflects the subsistent relations in the Trinity. Man's vocation on earth is to create similar subsistent relationships and thus live-in communion with God, with others and with all creatures (*LS* 240)[275]. Man's vocation is to bring the trinitarian dynamism, imprinted by God in all of us, into our relationships. Doing so allows us to develop an ecological spirituality founded on global solidarity. Our global solidarity with all of creation is due to our common eschatological destiny of being transformed and redeemed in Christ. Joshtrom Isaac Kureethadam writes "Creation has also a sublime eschatological destiny, namely, to be recapitulated in Christ in the fulness of time"[276].

---

[274] Pope Francis, *Laudato Si': On Care for Our Common Home*, London, Catholic Truth Society, 2015, p. 112.

[275] Ibid.

[276] Joshtrom Isaac Kureethadam, *The Ten Green Commandments of Laudato Si*, Minnesota, Liturgical Press, 1994, p. 176.

Models of Creation

Dominion Model

The source of the Dominion model of creation may be traced to literal reading of Genesis 1:26. When we read this passage of Scripture literally then it seems that God gives humans total control over the rest of creation. The ambiguity in the passage means that it is open to misinterpretation. Early Christian and medieval theologies presented an ordered and harmonious world view. Although creation is arranged in a hierarchy of being with the human person endowed with a rational soul at the apex, it is noteworthy that in early Christian and medieval thought the world was included in an ordered harmony with humanity before God. Even in the medieval period, dominion is understood as the normal use of creatures and the environment and not as total control.

The total dominion interpretation of Genesis stems from an anthropocentric turn in Protestant thought particularly evident in the attitude of Francis Bacon (1561 – 1626). A discriminating orthodox member of the Church of England, in his *Proficience and Advancement of learning* (1605), he insisted man's power to control nature was in his own hands[277]. He denied the existence of a *'summum bonum'*, the highest good to which all men are directed. For Francis Bacon, the Earth is a submissive object at man's disposal. He believed nature to be at the service of man, a slave to humanity[278]. According to Richard Bauckham, Francis Bacon hijacked the Genesis text to authorise the project of scientific knowledge and

---

[277] F.L. Cross (ed.) and E.A. Livingstone, *The Oxford Dictionary of the Christian Church*, Oxford, Oxford University Press, 1983, p. 120.

[278] Elizabeth A. Johnson, 'Losing and Finding Creation in the Christian Tradition', in Dieter T. Hessel and Rosemary Radford Ruether, *Christianity and Ecology*, Cambridge Massachusetts, Harvard University Press, 2000. p 10.

technological exploitation whose excesses, particularly in the last four centuries, have given us the ecological crisis. He writes… "The modern project of domination is indeed hubristic in that it aspired (and for technophilic progressivists still aspires) to the kind of control that had always thought to belong to God alone"[279]. This ideology is evident in Mormon communities in the United States where they subdued the land to build, what Donald Worster calls, a 'hydraulic society'[280]. Protestant theology was open to societal developments and often replaces the antiquated term 'dominion' with 'control'. It is obviously incorrect to read Genesis 1: 26 in isolation. It leads to attitudes expressed by reconstructionist preacher James Kennedy when he suggested to a convention of the Christian coalition in 1995 that true Christian citizenship means to take dominion over all things as vice-regents of God[281]. To establish the right relationship with our environment we need to read Genesis 1:26 within context and with reference to the other scriptural passages which set limits to dominion.

One passage from Scripture which warns us of the dangers of trying to dominate creation is the story of the Flood in Genesis 6-10. It is precisely the domination and the wickedness of humankind which causes God to regret his creation as he considers making a fresh start. Genesis 6-10 recounts an incomplete de-creation story and a temporary return to chaos. It is not necessary for God to completely make a fresh start because of one man, Noah. The hope for humanity is embodied in the person of Noah, a righteous man who with his family find favour with God. He is presented as an example of creation care and tasked with preservation of all that God has made. He is rewarded for his obedience with a continuation of the covenant relationship between God, creatures, and humanity. The covenant with Noah reinforces the divine command in Genesis 1: 29-30 that

---

[279] Richard Bauckham, *Bible and Ecology*, London, Darton Longman and Todd, 2019, p. 6 – 7.

[280] Robert B. Jackson, 'A False Dominion of Control', in in Kyle S. Van Houtan (ed) and Michael S. Northcott (ed), *Diversity and Dominion*, Oregon, Cascade Books, 2010, p. 110.

[281] Michael S. Northcott, 'The Dominion Lie: How Millennial Theology Erodes Creation Care' in Kyle S. Van Houtan (ed) and Michael S. Northcott (ed), *Diversity and Dominion*, Oregon, Cascade Books, 2010, p. 98.

the earth's resources are all of creation and not just humanity. The covenant serves to regulate the violence caused by 'all flesh'.

The three environmental miracles in Exodus 14-16 offer a right interpretation of 'dominion' in Genesis 1:26. With the Egyptians in pursuit of the Israelites, Moses stretches out his hand over the sea and divides it. After the Israelites have made their escape, Moses again stretches out his hand over the sea making it impossible for the Egyptians to pursue. Two months into the Exodus the Israelites being to starve in the desert and God performs the miracle of the mana in the Desert (Exod. 16:4). God limits the Israelites to taking only what they can eat. The result is the Israelites do not perish but survive. Next, Moses strikes the rock at Rephidim so that the people may drink (Exodus 17:6). Although we control the environment today in ways that were unthinkable in Biblical times, the Exodus reminds us that ultimately it is God who has the power over the natural laws. As the Israelites were commanded in the Desert to 'gather a day's portion every day' (Exodus 16:4), so must we only extract what we need form the environment even though technological advancements have given us the power of unlimited exploitation.

One scholar, Norman Habel, argues that God's answer to Job (Job 38:39 – 39:30) undermines the Genesis mandate for dominion[282]. God de-centres and re-orientates Job in the world. The story of Job in the Old Testament limits the concept of dominion and challenges anthropocentrism and hubris that maintains that dominion is the only relationship possible between humans and other creatures. God has created other animals with their own integrity and meaning. Job is not the apex of the animal world rather he is a creature, among others.

Scholars have debated over the connection between being made in the image and likeness of God and to have dominion over creation. In the last four centuries, a misinterpretation of 'dominion' has been the justification for humanity exercising power and control over creation and aspirations of omnipotence. Modern man has lost his sense of dependency in God. He desires to replace God with his ability to conquer the natural environment with technology. His

---

[282] Richard Bauckham, *Bible and Ecology*, London, Darton Longman and Todd, 2019, p. 51.

desire to reorder the God given order is often tyrannical and has brought the Earth to its limits. The original Judeo-Christian interpretation of 'dominion' is closer to humanity exercising control over creation on behalf of God rather than in place of God. It is closer to collaboration with and responsibility for creation rather than a total control over creation that leads to the extinction of certain species and the depletion of the earth's resources. This does not mean we are to restrict productive human enhancements such as gardens and art e.g., in Genesis 2:16 Adam tills and keeps the earth in the Garden of Eden.

Anthropology is primarily concerned with what it is to be a human being and Pope Francis criticizes tyrannical anthropocentrism in *Laudato Si'*. An anthropology which places humankind at the centre of everything is often used to justify our wanton use of the earth's resources. Dan Horan connects the 'anthropocentric privilege' to the exclusion of non-human world as part of the *Imago Dei* (Gen. 1:26)[283]. Anthropocentrism has had a negative effect on our self-understanding. The 'dominion model' finds its origins in the modern anthropocentric understanding of creation. Anthropocentrism diminishes the integrity of humanity within the *cosmos*, alienates humanity from the natural world and projects a reductionist view of nature. A few biblical references have had a disproportionate effect on our understanding of our role within the cosmos. If we are to develop a new ecological paradigm, to replace the existing technological paradigm, then ecology will need to be open to divine transcendence. The last five centuries have been characterised by technological advancements permitting mankind to shape the ecological processes he is a part of, often negatively. Anthropocentrism is at the heart of the dominion model of creation that has marred he twentieth century as modern humans seek total control over nature. Anthropocentrism has caused mankind to usurp the place of God in favour of higher productivity and profits. At the core of the technocratic paradigm is a selfish individualism. The reality is the fundamentalist interpretation of the dominion model is

---

[283] Dan Horan, *Deconstructing Anthropocentric Privilege: Imago Dei and Non-Human Agency,* in The Heythrop Journal, 60, 2019 cited in Dermot A. Lane, *Theology and Ecology,* Dublin, Messenger Publications, 2020, p. 33.

contrary to the Christian concept of community and the primacy of love (1 Corinthians 1-15).

The rise of the anthropocentric paradigm from the Enlightenment era caused a shift in the way humanity sees itself. The modern humanistic self is closed to the possibility of cosmic forces and transcendence. Un-belief, due to secularization, is the new normal. For various reasons, theology became anthropocentric. The current ecological crisis demands theology correct and reinterpret the dominion model of creation which has caused tyrannical anthropocentrism[284]. For this to happen theology will need to shift the focus from anthropocentrism to become theocentric. Theology will also need to redesign the hierarchical pyramid of being to a community circle of life which grasps the sacramental nature of the universe[285].

There is an obvious need to changes humanities utilitarian approach to the natural environment. Dermot A. Lane recommends a new paradigm to transform hierarchical dualisms underpinning anthropocentrism in theology. He suggests a first step would be to construct a theology of radical rationality reaching across the natural world and human beings. The role of the human community is to foster a sense of mutuality, reciprocity, and equality within relationships. The human community is at the centre of the theology of relationality. The second step is the development of a theology of embodiment both embodiment of the person and embodiment of the Earth. This includes the recognition that all experience is part of this embodiment. The third step is the recognition of what Teilhard de Chardin refers to as spirt-matter in the universe[286].

Climate change is causally related to the self-centred individualism of modern anthropocentrism[287]. It is also related to humanities self-understanding as the ecological crisis is a type of

---

[284] Dermot A. Lane, *Theology and Ecology,* Dublin, Messenger Publications, 2020, p. 32.

[285] Elizabeth A. Johnson, 'Losing and Finding Creation in the Christian Tradition', in Dieter T. Hessel and Rosemary Radford Ruether, *Christianity and Ecology*, Cambridge Massachusetts, Harvard University Press, 2000. p 15.

[286] Dermot A. Lane, *Theology and Ecology in Dialogue: The Wisdom of Laudato Si'*, Dublin, Messenger Publications, 2020, p. 35-36.

[287] Ibid., p. 41.

identity crisis related to what is means to be a human. The reality is we are not persons in isolation, our identity is dependent upon being in relation with other human beings and with our environment. The African concept of *Ubuntu* describes humanities interrelation as 'I am because we are'. The individualism of the twentieth century, and the loss of the concept of community, is at the root of the ecological crisis. Modern individualism has resulted in the alienation of the human from the natural world, the legitimization of exploitative attitudes and practices towards nature, isolation of the individual from the community of creation, the de-sacralisation of nature and dis-enchantment of the Universe[288].

The dominion model of creation presents a challenge for Christians in the light of Christ's passion, death, and resurrection for the sake of humanity as it is contrary to the Christian concept of community and the primacy of love (1 Corinthians 1-15). When we understand God as love then we understand the universe as a loving caress of God's love (*LS* 84)[289]. There is no mention of or evidence for the dominion model in the New Testament. The self-emptying of Christ in the Paschal Mystery, a model of *kenosis*, challenges our preconceived ideas of what it is to be fully human. The relational character of our humanity, as the three divine persons of the Trinity are 'subsistent relations'[290], causes us to reject all types of anthropocentrism; modern anthropocentrism (*LS, 115*), excessive anthropocentrism (*LS, 116*), tyrannical anthropocentrism (*LS, 68),* and misguided anthropocentrism (LS, 118, 119, 122)[291]. We are to favour theological anthropology grounded in a trinitarian theology of human identity.

---

[288] Dermot A. Lane, *Theology and Ecology in Dialogue: The Wisdom of Laudato Si'*, Dublin, Messenger Publications, 2020, p. 42.

[289] Pope Francis, *Laudato Si': On Care for Our Common Home*, London, Catholic Truth Society, 2015, p. 43.

[290] Gilles Emery O.P., *The Trinitarian Theology of St. Thomas Aquinas,* Oxford, Oxford University Press, 2007, p.15.

[291] Pope Francis, *Laudato Si': On Care for Our Common Home,* [website], 2015, Laudato si' (24 May 2015) | Francis (vatican.va), (accessed 28th December 2020).

Stewardship Model

The Stewardship model of creation is closer to the Judo-Christian attitude toward the environment than the modern technocratic paradigm. It is the foundation of Christian creation theology and Christian ecology. It is based upon both Genesis 1:28 and the injunction in Genesis 2: 15 that man is to till and keep the Garden of Eden. The Stewardship model of creation understands man's role as responsible stewardship of the environment in which he is held accountable to God. Dominion is extended to include dominion over himself, and not just the natural world, thus ensuring that his activity participates in the work of creation. Christian ecology interprets dominion as service within the *cosmos*. Pope John Paul II, discussing the difference between progress and threat writes...

> The essential meaning of this "kingship" and "dominion" of man over the visible world, which the creator himself gave man for his task, consists in the priority of ethics over technology, in the primacy of the person over things, and the superiority of the spirit over matter. Therefore, all phrases of present-day progress must be followed attentively[292].

The concept of responsible stewardship for the environment has featured significantly in the writings of Pope Benedict XVI. In a letter to his Holiness Bartholomew I in 2006, relating to the effect the deterioration of the Amazon environment is having on the indigenous population, he writes that the intrinsic connection between development, human need and the stewardship of creation is more important now than ever[293]. He echoes this sentiment in a letter on the Arctic region to the Patriarch of Constantinople in 2007, when he writes that there is a pressing need for science and religion to work together to safeguard the gifts of nature to promote responsible stewardship[294]. This may only be achieved with sustainable development which necessitates an affirmation of the vital relationship between the ecology of the human person and the

---

[292] Pope John Paul II, *Redemptor Hominis*, [website], 1979, Redemptor Hominis (4 March 1979) | John Paul II (vatican.va), (accessed 29th December 2020).

[293] Pope Benedict XVI, *The Garden of God: Toward a Human Ecology*, Washington, The Catholic University of America Press, 2014, p. 11.

[294] Ibid., p. 19.

ecology of nature[295]. In his general audience in 2009, Pope Benedict XVI comments that the intrinsic order of creation guides us in how we are to be responsible stewards. He connects environmental concern with the theme of integral human development and the need for responsible stewardship to preserve the environment for future generations. He writes …

> The created world, structured in an intelligent way by God, is entrusted to our responsibility and though we are able to analyse and transform it we cannot consider ourselves creation's absolute master. We are called, rather, to exercise responsible stewardship of creation, in order to protect it, to enjoy its fruits, and to cultivate it, finding the resources necessary for everyone to live with dignity. Through the help of nature itself and through hard work and creativity, humanity is indeed capable of carrying out its grave duty to hand on the earth to future generations so that they too, in turn, will be able to inhabit it worthily and continue to cultivate it[296].

Pope Benedict understands God's command in Genesis 1:28 as a summons to responsibility and not as the permission to exploit creation over the desire to have dominion over it[297]. This, in-fact, leads only to conflict (Genesis 3:17-19). As the original harmony is disrupted by the refusal of Adam and Eve to be God's creatures and their desire to take the place of God, so do we provoke rebellion on the part of nature when we use it arbitrarily. Pope Benedict states that man has a duty to exercise responsible stewardship over creation. Failure to do so causes extra hardship for large numbers of people in different countries. We are also duty bound to find the proper use and place for technology. Pope Benedict XVI does not advocate staking everything on technology as to believe it is the exclusive agent of happiness. This brings a reification of the human person and leads to

---

[295] Pope Benedict XVI, *For the Celebration of the World Day of Peace*, [Website], 2007, 40th World Day of Peace 2007, The Human Person, the Heart of Peace | BENEDICT XVI (vatican.va), (accessed 29th December 2020).

[296] Pope Benedict XVI, General Audience, [Website], 2009, General Audience of 26 August 2009: Safeguarding of Creation | BENEDICT XVI (vatican.va), (accessed 29th December 2020).

[297] Pope Benedict XVI, *Message of Holiness Pope Benedict XVI: For the Celebration of the World Day of Peace*, [Website], 2010, 43rd World Day of Peace 2010, If You Want to Cultivate Peace, Protect Creation | BENEDICT XVI (vatican.va), (29th December 2020).

unhappiness when powers it does not possess are not attributed to it. Technology that dominates human beings deprives them of their humanity[298].

The 'Stewardship' model of creation is an improvement to the 'Dominion' model of creation and offers an alternative to the exploitation produced by the dominion model. However, many scholars such as Denis Edwards, Richard Bauckham Elizabeth Johnson, and Dan Horan have found the underlying assumptions of the stewardship model to be problematic. Dermot A. Lane emphasises this when he writes…

> They neglect the interdependence of the human species with the rest of life in earth; they see the human as independent and external and separate from the rest of creation; they establish a vertical, top-down relationship between humans and other creatures (effectively a hangover from the dominion model); they give humans a responsible mastery over other creatures, making them mere passive recipients[299].

Dermot A. Lane criticises the stewardship model for promoting the anthropocentrism of the dominion model giving human beings the free use of the creatures of creation. He states that in practice the stewardship model is dualistic and hierarchical[300]. Richard Bauckham states that the stewardship model does provide a strong alternative to dominion model although it has distinct unspoken limitations[301]. He outlines five criticisms of the stewardship model of creation. The first is based on Lovelock's theory of 'Gaia', that all life is a single self-regulating system that operates to sustain the habitability of the earth. Due to an unconscious hubris humanity does not have the knowledge or the capacity to achieve the goals of

---

[298] Pope Benedict XVI, Address of His Holiness Benedict XVI To Six New Ambassadors Accredited to the Holy See, [website], 2011, To the new Ambassadors accredited to the Holy See on the occasion of the presentation of the Letters of Credence (June 9, 2011) | BENEDICT XVI (vatican.va), (accessed 29th December 2020).

[299] Dermot A. Lane, *Theology and Ecology in Dialogue: The Wisdom of Laudato Si'*, Dublin, Messenger Publications, 2020, p. 123.

[300] Ibid.

[301] Richard Bauckham, *Bible and Ecology: Rediscovering the Community of Creation*, London, Darton, Longman and Todd Ltd, 2010, p. 2.

responsible stewardship[302]. Lovelock states that if the concept of Gaia is true, and the Earth is a self-regulating system, then stewardship is a hubristic attempt to do what Gaia is doing and has been doing for millions of years. This sentiment is echoed by Clare Palmer when she states we have limited and partial control over the earth's complex ecosystems and atmospheric conditions. Modern scientific-technological projects which seek to provide a technological-fix to the climate crisis leads us to a point where technology will either replace or modify human nature itself to the extent of creating a new species. The problem is human knowledge and power does not give us controlling power over the earth therefore our stewardship is limited.

The second criticism levelled by Richard Bauckham is that human stewardship neglects God's continuing involvement in creation. The stewardship model of creation suggests God created the world and then delegated its governance to humanity. This creates a theological problem for Christians as it indicates God's role in creation ended with the creation of humanity. Contemplation of the paschal mystery leads us to understand God is constantly active in salvation history. Humans, therefore, should care for creation in the context of God's own caring for it and not in place of God's caring for creation[303].

The third criticism of the stewardship model of creation as outlined by Richard Bauckham is that the stewardship model lacks specific content and is therefore open to different interpretations. For example, in the seventeenth century, stewardship is interpreted as humanity controlling creation for creations good. In the seventeenth century creation is understood to be a mess that needs to be cleared up and put in order. Whereas the twentieth century Christian interpretation of stewardship is that it is to preserve creation from damage being done to it and to change and intervene is to ruin it. The subtle difference is the seventeenth century interpretation of stewardship, as professed by Francis Bacon and Matthew Hale, implies creation needs us. The twentieth century interpretation

---

[302] Richard Bauckham, *Bible and Ecology: Rediscovering the Community of Creation*, London, Darton, Longman and Todd Ltd, 2010, p. 3.

[303] Ibid, p. 8.

implies we are responsible for destroying the natural harmony of creation and we have the responsibility to rectify the damage caused through our interference. Creation existed before the existence of humanity and does not need the tyranny of pretended divine power[304].

The fourth criticism of the stewardship model of creation as outlined by Richard Bauckham, is that it depicts humanities relation to other creatures in a vertical way without taking the corresponding horizontal relationship with God into consideration. This is essentially a criticism of the hierarchy of creation where humanity is placed above non-humans in the hierarchy and God is placed above both humanity and non-humans. The stewardship model of creation denies the creatureliness of humanity. St. Ignatius of Loyola writes in his contemplation to attain the love of God...

> This is to reflect on how God dwells in creatures: in the elements giving them existence, in the plants giving them life, in the animals conferring on them sensation, in man bestowing understanding. So, he dwells in me and gives me being, life, sensation, intelligence; and makes a temple of me, since I am created in the likeness and image of Divine Majesty[305].

St. Ignatius reflects on the divine gift of life within all of creation including humanity. The stewardship model suggests a one-way relationship between humanity and the rest of creation which is devoid of any reciprocity. According to Bauckham, the exclusive focus on the vertical relationship to the rest of creation, whether we refer to it as dominion, stewardship or even priesthood, is the ideological driving force of the modern technological project to dominate nature[306]. A concept of stewardship which denies our dependence upon and embeddedness within the rest of creation leads us only to a one-sided vertical relationship and does not fully capture

---

[304] Richard Bauckham, *Bible and Ecology: Rediscovering the Community of Creation*, London, Darton, Longman and Todd Ltd, 2010, p. 10.

[305] St. Ignatius of Loyola, *Spiritual Exercises*, Flavigny-sur-Ozerain, Traditions Monastiques, 2007, p. 104.

[306] Richard Bauckham, *Bible and Ecology: Rediscovering the Community of Creation*, London, Darton, Longman and Todd Ltd, 2010, p. 11.

the complexity and intricacies of humanities relationship with creation.

The fifth and final criticism of the stewardship model of creation, offered by Richard Bauckham, is that the model is founded upon isolated scriptural texts namely Genesis 1: 26, 28 and Genesis 2:15. It is important to interpret these passages of scripture within the wider Biblical theme of humanities role within God's creation. It is essential to consider all scriptural reference to creation if we are to develop proper ecological hermeneutic.

We may say that the stewardship model of creation is an alternative and an improvement to the dominion model of creation however it falls short in describing an authentic Christian attitude toward creation and the environment. A genuine Christian model of creation will understand dominion in the broader Biblical theologies of creation found within the prophets, the Psalms, and the book of Job[307]. Both Dermot Lane and Richard Bauckham identifies the 'Community' model of creation also known as the 'Kinship' model of creation as the authentic Christian model of creation.

Kinship Model – Community of Creation

The community model of creation finds its roots in the creation theology of the Old Testament. Modern use of the term 'community' to describe the interrelation between humans and creatures in eco-systems originates in the work of Aldo Leopold, the America conservationist[308]. The kinship-community model differs from the dominion and stewardship model of creation in being theocentric rather than anthropocentric. This means that there is no place in worship for one creature over another. This model teaches that although we are made in the image of God and have been tasked with tilling the earth and keeping it (Genesis 2:15) we too are part of the community of creatures orientated to God our common creator.

---

[307] Dermot A. Lane, *Theology and Ecology in Dialogue: The Wisdom of Laudato Si'*, Dublin, Messenger Publications, 2020, p. 123.

[308] Richard Bauckham, *Bible and Ecology: Rediscovering the Community of Creation*, London, Darton, Longman and Todd Ltd, 2010, p. 87.

Examples of the community model of creation may be found in in the Old Testament in Job 38-39 and Psalm 104.

Job chapter 38 begins questioning Job's identity. Who is Job, is he is a rival to Yahweh? The Earth is pictured as a building planned by an architect where a surveyor mapped out the site and the foundations and corner stone where laid. The sea is described as a baby which needed Yahweh's loving care. The first number of strophes confirm the supremacy of the Lord Yahweh. There are eight creatures described in Job 38:39 – 39:30; the lion, the raven, the hawk, the eagle, the mountain goat, the wild donkey, the wild ox, and war horse. It is Yahweh, and not Job, who nourishes and cares for these creatures. Psalm 104 is more subtle in putting humanity in its place when compared with Job 38-39[309]. This hymn of praise acknowledges Yahweh as the creator who providentially maintains the inhabitable world. The Psalm is structured into four parts vs 1-9 the creation of the world, vs 10-18 the provision of water, vs 19-26 the creation of moon and sun and acquisition of food by day and night, and vs 27-35 a prayer for rain. It is Yahweh who is the source of the breath of life and provides water, food, habitat, and the times and seasons. Yahweh's joy in his creation finds expression in the repeated sending of the rains. This in turn brings joy to the Israelites who are dependent upon the rains for agriculture. God's creation is not utilitarian in its purpose (v. 31). God creates the world so all his creatures may participate in his joy which extends to the birds of the air who sing in their branches (v. 12), to humanity with wine and bread to gladden and strengthen their hearts and oil to make his face shine (v.15). The great sea monster Leviathan is created by God to play in the ocean (v 26.) Leviathan is a representation of the chaos formed by God in Genesis 1. The central message is all of creation is dependent upon God and empowered by God. The animals named in the Psalm are beyond human control. Humanity is included in God's providential care and is part of the diversity of creation. In Psalm 104, humanity is not reigning supreme over creation as this place is reserved for God alone. The Psalm is theocentric, stressing the dependence of human and non-human creation on God's providential

---

[309] Richard Bauckham, *Bible and Ecology: Rediscovering the Community of Creation*, London, Darton, Longman and Todd Ltd, 2010, p. 65.

care. It lays the foundation for the Community/ Kinship Model of creation.

An example of the Kinship Model of creation may also be found in the New Testament in the Sermon on the Mount in Matthew 6: 25-33. In the Sermon on the Mount, Jesus teaches his disciples the role of humanity within God's creation. The sermon is based on the creation theology of the Old Testament contained in Psalm 104 in the Hebrew Bible. The idolatry of common basic human needs such as eating, drinking, and clothing have caused the disciples of Christ to be anxious (*merimnaō*). Their focus on their own efforts, rather than on their dependence on the resources of creation, is the cause of their anxiety. The anxiety of the apostles causes them to have a crisis of faith in divine providence. Jesus' teaching, a combination of wisdom theology and eschatology, is a radical development of the dominion and stewardship models of creation from Genesis one and two. He teaches his disciples to have faith in divine providence for their day - to - day material needs. Jesus teaches the image of God as a wise and generous creator who loves and preserves his creation. He compares the way in which the birds of the air are provided for, yet they do not store or process their food, with the way in which humans focus on their own labour. The focus on Yahweh God's providential care for creation and our dependence on the creator, is Jesus' way of alleviating the disciples fear of not having enough. Jesus challenges us to place ourselves within creation and to trust in divine providence. If God provides for the birds of the air and the lilies of the field, this is a guarantee he will provide for the pinnacle of his creation, humanity. When humanity participates in the community of God's creation then God given resources are equally shared. Jesus' teaching demands radical faith in divine providence. It is liberating as, for Jesus, the priority is the building up of the Kingdom of God through social justice. He compares those who prioritise food, clothing, and the body to foreigners (*gentiles*).

The Sermon on the mount is a challenge to our twenty- first century lifestyle. We, like the disciples, are anxious. Our anxiety is to maintain our affluent lifestyles. There exists belief in the West that rapid economic growth will solve social problems as the new wealth will trickle down to the poorer sectors of society[310]. This is of course a misleading idea. Our obsessive consumption to maintain our lifestyles is depleting the earth's resources. What is more, not everyone on the earth has what they need for basic subsistence. There is a real and urgent need for humanity to re-establish our role within the community of God's creation by living within sustainable ecological limits. Jesus instructed humanity to prioritise the building up of the Kingdom of Heaven. *Jesus Christ* makes the point that if God provides immediately and obviously for sparrows, when we place ourselves within the community of creation, we are no less dependent on the Creator. When we do so we negate the mastery and anthropocentricity of the dominion and stewardship models of creation. The Kinship model of creation depends on participation in the community of creation and trust in God's providential care. Jesus gives us a new way of seeing, and points to the abundance of the earth's resources for all. This is a direct challenge to the reductionist view of creation and the modern excess fuelled by the process of globalisation. Pope Benedict XVI writes…

> In nature, the believer recognises the wonderful result of God's creative activity, which we may use responsibly to satisfy our legitimate needs, material or otherwise, while respecting the intrinsic balance of creation. If this vision is lost, we end up seeing nature as an untouchable taboo, or on the contrary abusing it. Neither attitude is consonant with the Christian vision of nature as the fruit of God's creation[311].

The 'Community' model of creation represents a retrieval of the original Biblical vision of the community of creation[312]. The presence of an animating and renewing Spirit in human and non-human creation testifies to an omnipresent, life-giving force, theists refer to as the Holy Spirit. Our Greek Orthodox brothers are very learned in the field of pneumatology and from whom we may learn. For the Greek Orthodox Church, the entire world is an Icon engraved

---

[310] Donal Dorr, *Option for the Poor: A Hundred Years of Vatican Social Teaching*, Dublin, Gill and Macmillan Ltd, 1983, p. 94, 95.

[311] Pope Benedict XVI, *Caritas In Veritate*, [website], 2009, Caritas in veritate (June 29, 2009) | BENEDICT XVI (vatican.va), (accessed 2nd January 2021).

[312] Dermot A. Lane, *Theology and Ecology in Dialogue: The Wisdom of Laudato Si'*, Dublin, Messenger Publications, 2020, p. 124.

by the unique iconographer of the Word of God, namely the Holy Spirit. John Chryssavgis writes... "So, if, indeed, there exists today a vision that can transcend – perhaps trans-form all national and denominational tensions, it may well be that our environment is understood as a sacrament of the Spirit. The breath of the Spirit brings out the sacramentality of nature and bestows on it the fragrance of resurrection[313].

The omnipresent divine spirit in all things, human and non-human, adds a sacramental element to creation itself. This is evident in the Genesis 1 which climaxes with the creation of the Sabbath. The 'Community of Creation' model replaces a hierarchy of creation with notions of kinship i.e., human beings are not above other creatures but are fellow creatures on a journey. Humans become 'insiders' with a moral responsibility in the community model of creation[314]. All of creation is interconnected and interdependent. The concept of the relational character of everything in the universe is expressed by Pope Francis in *Laudato Si'* when he writes "Everything is interconnected, and this invites us to develop a spirituality of that global solidarity which flows from the mystery of the Trinity"[315]. The community model of creations adopts an ascending model to describe the action of the Trinity in creation. The Spirit is involved in creation from the beginning.

The 'Community Model' of creation is founded upon the concept of reciprocity and not competition. This concept causes us to re-evaluate our understanding of humanity. The human exists within the community of creation. Humanity shares both their origins and their destinations with other creatures. This is not to diminish the uniqueness of humanity rather to acknowledge the theo-centricism of creation. St. Thomas Aquinas writes...

---

[313] John Chryssavgis, 'The World of Icon and Creation: An Orthodox Perspective on Ecology and Pneumatology' in Dieter D. Hessel (ed) and Rosemary Radford Ruether (ed), Chri*stianity and Ecology*, Massachusetts, Harvard University Press, 2000, p.91.

[314] Dermot A. Lane, *Theology and Ecology in Dialogue: The Wisdom of Laudato Si'*, Dublin, Messenger Publications, 2020, p. 125.

[315] Pope Francis, *Laudato Si': On Care for Our Common Home*, [website], 2015, Laudato si' (24 May 2015) | Francis (vatican.va), (accessed 3rd January 2021).

Hence, we must say that the distinction and multitude of things come from the intention of the first agent, who is God. For he brought things into being in order that his goodness might be communicated to creatures and be represented by them; and because his goodness could not be adequately represented by one creature alone, he produced many and diverse creatures, that what was wanting to one in the representation of the divine goodness might be supplied by another. For goodness which in God is simple and unform, in creatures is manifold and divided and hence the whole universe participates the divine goodness more perfectly, and represents it better than any single creature whatever[316].

In the theocentric universe there is respect for the diversity of creation and reciprocity between the members of the community. Each member of the community shares its origin in the creator and is in turn orientated toward God. Pope Francis, in *Laudato Si'*, emphasizes this does not deprive humanity of their unique worth and tremendous responsibility. It also does not imply a divinization of the earth that prevents us from working on it and protecting it in its fragility[317]. Richard Bauckham states… "Our creation in the image of God and the unique dominion given to us do not abolish our fundamental community with other creatures. The vertical does not cancel the horizontal"[318].Calvin B. Dewitt makes a distinction between the two-party relationship of the dominion and stewardship models of creation and the three-party relationship of the community of creation model[319].

---

[316] St. Thomas Aquinas, *Summa Theologica*, [website], St. Thomas Aquinas: Summa Theologica - Christian Classics Ethereal Library (ccel.org), (accessed 3rd January 2020).

[317] Pope Francis, Laudato Si', [website], 2015, Laudato si' (24 May 2015) | Francis (vatican.va), (accessed 3rd January 2021).

[318] Richard Bauckham, *Bible and Ecology: Rediscovering the Community of Creation*, London, Darton Longman and Todd, 2019, p. 31.

[319] Calvin B. Dewitt, 'Behemoth and Batrachians in the Eye of God: Responsibility to Other Kinds in Biblical Perspective', in Dieter D. Hessel (ed) and Rosemary Radford Ruether (ed), Chr*istianity and Ecology*, Massachusetts, Harvard University Press, 2000, p. 297.

The three-party relationship may be represented in a diagram:

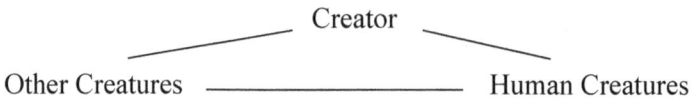

Creator

Other Creatures ———————————— Human Creatures

As with Job, when we see other creatures through the eyes of their Creator then we add another dimension to the human – non-human relationship. We see non-human creatures as an integral part of creation and nature as a habitat for God's creatures. The authority over things belongs to the Author of life and we have no authority to destroy what we did not create. This would be paramount to an onlooker, beholder or a curator destroying a masterpiece of art. The value of non-human creation is not derived from their utility, market price, cuteness or charm but their value is derived from the creator e.g. a hawk is not created for man's use but has a beauty and grace humanity can appreciate[320]. In Genesis 1 God declared all of creation good and humanity to be very good. It is essential to incorporate the divine dimension into the community model of creation to illuminate the human – non-human relationship. Richard Bauckham states we join our fellow-creatures in attributing glory to God there is no hierarchy and anthropocentricity. When we recognise creation is praising God we abandon the instrumental view of nature. We glimpse the value of other creatures to God that has nothing to do with their usefulness to us[321]. The community model of creation is a community circle of interdependent kinship.

---

[320] Calvin B. Dewitt, 'Behemoth and Batrachians in the Eye of God: Responsibility to Other Kinds in Biblical Perspective', in Dieter D. Hessel (ed) and Rosemary Radford Ruether (ed), Chri*stianity and Ecology*, Massachusetts, Harvard University Press, 2000, p. 297 – 298.

[321] Richard Bauckham, *Bible and Ecology*, London, Darton Longman and Todd, 2019, p. 80.

St. Francis of Assisi:
A Model of Ecological Conversion

Monasticism and Creation

The Judeo-Christian view of creation has always taught that the *cosmos* is man's natural home. The theological tradition within the church has always fostered respect for creation. This is also found in antiquity and is evident in non-Christian antique poets such as Ausonius (c. 310 - 395). In his poem Moselle, he celebrates the beauty of the river Moselle. Christian philosophers such as St. Augustine (354- 430) provided the foundation for the Christian world view and succeeded in integrating classical and original philosophic interpretations of creation. St. Augustine stated the beauty and utility of natural creation is bestowed with divine generosity on man even though he is cast from paradise. He is amazed at the diversity within creation with countless different species. He lists the many different colours of the sea and the pleasure we get from being on dry land when it is stormy. Of food and medicine, he writes...

> Think too of the abundant supply of food everywhere to satisfy our hunger, the variety of flavours to suit our pampered taste, lavishly distributed by the riches of nature, not produced by the skill and labour of cooks! Think, too, of all the resources for the preservation of health, or its restoration, the welcome alternation of the day and night, the soothing coolness of the breezes, and all the material for clothing provided by plants and animals. Who could give a complete list of all these natural blessings?[322]

Early ascetic movements, from the time of St. Anthony (c. 251 - 356) and St. Basil (329 - 379), are characterised by an

---

[322] Saint Augustine, *City of God*, London, Penguin Books, 2003, p. 1075.

appreciation for creation. St. Basil believed contemplation of creation inspired humility. The Irish *Peregrini*, from the 5th to the 9th Century, redefined the ascetic life combining wandering pilgrimage with a deep connection to the natural environment. The Celtic Saints love for birds and beasts is evident in Adomnán's story of 'The Lost Bird' contained in his collection of Saint Colum Cille's prophecies. The story recalls after establishing his foundation on Iona, Saint Colum Cille prophesied to one of the brothers that an exhausted Crane will arrive to the west of the Island from the north of Ireland within three days. St. Colum Cille foretold to a brother that the Crane will fall on the shore and the brother will carefully lift the Crane and take it to a nearby house. The brother is ordered to nurse and care for the Crane. After three days the Crane will be restored to good health and return to the north of Ireland, St. Colum Cille's native home. St. Adomnán assures the reader that everything took place as Saint Column Cille had foretold indicating the Irish Saints connection with the non-human world[323]. The *Voyage of St. Brendan*, a story recounting the exploration of the natural world by Irish Monks, was popular throughout Europe in the 9th Century. According to Armstrong it is possible the Irish *Peregrini* directly influenced St. Francis and the Franciscans. There are certainly similarities between the Irish and Franciscan ascetic traditions and their appreciation of sacredness of creation.

The middle-ages are characterised by a zeal within the Church to return to an authentic apostolic Christianity. The scientific or philosophic attitude toward creation in the middle-ages linked creation and the Creator with symbolism, as the Christian encyclopaedists such as Isidore passed on classical science e.g., astronomical observations and calendrical data[324]. However, at this time, the relationship between faith and science began to break down and diverge. With the age of the enlightenment, scientists no longer evaluated the technological application of science according to the moral truths of the Church. According to Paul Haffner… "Precisely this lack of moral consciousness lies at the root of current

---

[323] Desmond Forristal, *Colum Cille: The Fox and the Dove*, Dublin, Veritas, 1997, p. 53 – 54.

[324] Rodger D. Sorrell, *St. Francis of Assisi, and Nature: Tradition and Innovation in Western Christian Attitudes towards the Environment*, Oxford, Oxford University Press, 1988, p. 12.

environmental problems, and hence the expression 'From Assisi to Bikini' encapsulates the contrast between the medieval and twentieth century approaches to creation"[325]. Modern science is characterised with a pantheistic view of creation which discourages natural and revealed transcendent laws of the *cosmos*.

Ascetic suspicion of creation seems to be the exception in middle-ages rather than the rule as monastic settlements during the Middle Ages fostered a deep appreciation towards creation. The location of monastic settlements was often in areas of outstanding and enchanting natural beauty[326]. Pope John Paul II, writing in his message for World Day of Peace in 1990, highlights the way in which Franciscan spirituality has witnessed to the kinship of man with his creaturely environment fostering in him an attitude of respect for every reality in the surrounding world[327]. Both Saint Benedict and Saint Francis have taught respect for creation. For Saint Benedict both the Scriptures and creation are the word of God. The singing of the Psalms in the Benedictine tradition filled the monks with a love for creation (Psalm 41, 148). Their recitation of the Psalms is in tune with the seasons[328]. St. Benedict encouraged an active approach to the environment encouraging the monks to live from the work of their hands[329]. Common themes in the middle-aged monasticism are humility, obedience, manually labour, learning, stewardship, and community. St. Francis encouraged a concrete brotherhood of creation and humanity

We will examine in more detail the Franciscan attitude toward creation. We learn of St. Francis' sensitised connection with creation from the writings of his first hagiographer Brother Thomas Celano (d. 1260). St. Francis lived an ascetic life often praying in a cave and

---

[325] Paul Haffner, *Mystery of Creation*, Herefordshire, Gracewing, 1995, p. 294.

[326] Rodger D. Sorrell, *St. Francis of Assisi, and Nature: Tradition and Innovation in Western Christian Attitudes towards the Environment*, Oxford, Oxford University Press, 1988, p. 15.

[327] Pope John Paul II, *Peace with God the Creator, Peace with all of Creation*, [Website], 1990, http://www.vatican.va/content/john-paul-ii/en/messages/peace/documents/hf_jp-ii_mes_19891208_xxiii-world-day-for-peace.html, (accessed 25th December, 2010).

[328] Timothy Fry (ed.), *The Rule of St. Benedict in English*, Minnesota, The Liturgical Press, 1982, p.40.

[329] Ibid., p.69-70.

travelling half clothed. Brother Celano provides an account of St. Francis in Greccio when a brother brought him a live rabbit caught in a trap. When St. Francis saw the rabbit, he was moved by tenderness and asked the rabbit "Why did you let yourself get caught?". When the brother released the rabbit, the rabbit took shelter in the bosom of St. Francis without any prompting. And any time it was released it rushed back to St. Francis' lap. St. Francis often threw fish back when they were caught. One time in a boat at the port of Lake Rieti a fisherman caught a large fish and gave it to the Saint. He accepted it and calling it brother he put it in the water next to the little boat and blessed it with devotion in the name of the Lord. The fish did not swim away but stayed next to the boat playing in the water until the Holy man gave it permission to leave. Br Thomas Celano writes...

> Thus, the glorious father Francis, walking in the way of obedience, and embracing the yoke of complete submission to God, was worthy of the great honour before God of having the obedience of creatures. He is truly a saint, whom creatures obey in this way: at his wish, the very elements convert themselves to other uses[330].

St. Francis had deep sense of concern not only for humanity but also for mute, brute animals including reptiles, birds, and all other creatures. He had a special fondness for lambs since in the Scriptures the Lord's humility is compared to the lamb. On the road toward Osimo he came upon a Shepherd in the fields pasturing a flock of goats. St. Francis saw one little sheep walking among the goats. He said to his companion Brother Paul, the little sheep is like Lord *Jesus Christ* walking among the Pharisees and the chief priests. A travelling merchant bought the Lamb for the brothers and they gifted it to maidservants of Christ in the cloister of San Severino. The maidservants made a tunic from its wool and gifted it to St. Francis. St. Francis' love for creation stems from his deep affection for all things belonging to God. In contemplating God's creatures, he

---

[330] Regis J. Armstrong. O.F.M. Cap.(ed.), J. A. Wayne Hellman, O.F.M. Conv.(ed.), William J. Short, O.F.M. (ed.), St. Francis of Assisi the Saint: Early Documents, New York, New City Press, 1999, p. 236.

realized the wisdom, power, and goodness of the Creator[331]. It is his humility before God that causes him to savour the sweetness of God's Creation including the Sun, the Moon, and the Stars in the Sky. All of creation caused him to praise and glorify the Creator. Even gazing at flowers caused St. Francis to rejoice. He is even known to have preached to flowers inviting them to praise the Lord as if they had reason. He called all creatures brothers and sisters.

We can identify the distinctive characteristic of the Franciscan attitude toward creation. Francis' attitude toward nature relates to his ascetic lifestyle as his complete submission to divine providence taught St. Francis and his followers a profound humility. He often pointed to our Lord's retreat to the desert as an example of how creation can be the place where we retreat to meet God. Undoubtedly, it is Francis' choice to live the ascetic life and often retreat to isolated locations that caused him to have deep appreciation and connection with creation. Despite Francis' positive attitude, the environment also could be a place where evil resided and the source of torture and temptation. Julian of Speyer (1232-1235) in 'The Life of Saint Francis', recounts how St. Francis sought out solitary places in the wilderness. In these places he endured many terrors of the devil, being tempted with thoughts that endangered his mortal soul. Solitary places provided St. Francis with the wisdom to fight hand to hand against the devil and he taught others to do the same[332].

St. Francis' 'Sermon to the Birds' and 'Canticle of Creatures' help us understand how he redefined the ascetic's relationship with creation and represent a major contribution to our understanding of the 'Community' model of creation. We will see how St. Francis's love for creation, the poor and ecology make him the perfect model of integral ecology[333].

---

[331] Regis J. Armstrong. O.F.M. Cap.(ed.), J. A. Wayne Hellman, O.F.M. Conv.(ed.), William J. Short, O.F.M. (ed.), St. Francis of Assisi the Saint: Early Documents, New York, New City Press, 1999, p. 250.

[332] Ibid., p. 408.

[333] Joshtrom Isaac Kureethadam, *The Ten Commandments of Laudato Si'*, Minnesota, Liturgical Press, 2015, p.126.

St. Francis' Sermon to the Birds: Transcendence of Tradition

Brother Thomas Celano (d. 1260) gives an account of St. Francis travelling through the Spoleto valley. At a place near Bevagna, a great multitude of Bird of different types gathered. When Francis saw the Birds, he ran towards them leaving the other Brothers at the side of the road. Br. Thomas Celano tells us … 'He was a Man of great fervour, feeling much sweetness and tenderness even towards lesser, irrational creatures'[334]. He greeted them and the Birds did not take flight. He began to preach to the Birds advising them to praise and love the creator. He said to them that God made them noble, provided for them and protects them. On hearing St. Francis' words, the Birds rejoiced, and Francis blessed them before giving them permission to fly away. Then St. Francis and the other brothers went on their way rejoicing. Brother Celano tells us from that day onwards he exhorted all creatures to give praise to God. On another occasion St. Francis went to a village called Alviano to preach. He went to a high place and asked for silence. Many swallows nesting there began to shriek and chirp. St. Francis said "My sister swallows, now it is time for me to speak, since you have already said enough. Listen to the word of the Lord and stay quiet and calm until the word of the Lord is completed[335]. The little Birds fell silent immediately and all presents were filled with wonder at St. Francis' holiness and rushed toward him to touch his clothes. Both of these sermon accounts are controversial and represent an attempt by St. Francis to restore the apostolic way of life. There is no account of anyone before St. Francis addressing the non-human natural world in a homiletic manner. He confronts creation and includes it the plan of salvation thus restoring the Gospel ideal[336]. The hagiographer, Celano, is indicating to the reader St. Francis is participating in the apostolic age and extending the gospel message to all of creation. Creation has

---

[334] Regis J. Armstrong. O.F.M. Cap.(ed.), J. A. Wayne Hellman, O.F.M. Conv.(ed.), William J. Short, O.F.M. (ed.), St. Francis of Assisi the Saint: Early Documents, New York, New City Press, 1999, p. 234.

[335] Ibid., p. 235.

[336] Rodger D. Sorrell, *St. Francis of Assisi, and Nature: Tradition and Innovation in Western Christian Attitudes towards the Environment,* Oxford, Oxford University Press, 1988, p. 62.

its own special niche and status in God's eyes justifying respect and reciprocity between human and non-human creation.

St. Francis' Vision: Canticle of Creatures

St. Francis' interpretation of the Scriptures and the Psalms caused him to be a reformer and innovator. Interestingly he never uses the word nature (natura) rather talks about the 'heavens', 'the earth', 'the world', and 'all creatures under the heavens'[337]. Franciscan monasteries are historically one place where respect for creation has flourished. Pope John Paul II officially recognised this in *Inter Santos* when he proclaimed St. Francis the patron Saint of growers of Ecology[338]. Pope Francis, in *Laudato Si'*, refers to St. Francis as the example par excellence of care for the vulnerable and of an integral ecology lived out joyfully and authentically (LS 10)[339]. St. Francis had an awareness that our daily use of Lord's creatures greatly offends the Creator. As we cannot live without the Lord's creatures, he wished to compose a new hymn of praise. When we read the 'Canticle of Creatures' (1225) we find it is St. Francis who gives the proper place to the Creator. The poetic praise of God reveals Francis' vision of God, creation, and the human soul[340]. Pope Benedict XVI, in his message for the celebration of the Fortieth World Day of Peace, referred to the poem prayer of St. Francis as a wonderful and timely example of the multifaceted ecology[341]. St. Francis teaches us what it means to be truly human through his triple

---

[337] Rodger D. Sorrell, *St. Francis of Assisi, and Nature: Tradition and Innovation in Western Christian Attitudes towards the Environment*, Oxford, Oxford University Press, 1988, p. 7.

[338] Pope John Paul II, *Inter Sanctos Proclamation of St. Francis of Assisi as Patron of Ecology*, [website], 1979, Carta apostólica Inter sanctos para la proclamación de San Francisco de Asís como Patrono de la Ecología (29 de noviembre de 1979) | Juan Pablo II (vatican.va), (accessed 28th November 2011).

[339] Pope Francis, *Laudato Si'*, London, Catholic Truth Society, 2015, p.11.

[340] Regis J. Armstrong. O.F.M. Cap.(ed.), J. A. Wayne Hellman, O.F.M. Conv.(ed.), William J. Short, O.F.M. (ed.), St. Francis of Assisi the Saint: Early Documents, New York, New City Press, 1999, p. 113.

[341] Pope Benedict XVI, *Message of his Holiness Pope Benedict XVI For the Celebration of World Day of Peace: The Human Person, The Heart of Peace*, (The Holy See: Papal Archive 2007) 40th World Day of Peace 2007, The Human Person, the Heart of Peace | BENEDICT XVI (vatican.va).

conversion and love for the poor, the whole of creation and ultimately the Creator. He is a model of integral ecology because of his ability to transcend the language of biology and mathematic to the language of praise and worship[342]. The theology of the kinship-community model of creation is evident in the 'Canticle of Creatures'. In the first part of the Canticle Creatures (vs 1-9) the Saint sings the praises of creation in Glorifying God. Verse 10-11 were composed after a quarrel between civil and religious authorities in Assisi. The final verses 12-13 were composed on Francis' death bed, with verse 14 possibly being a refrain (see annex 1).

Two years before the composition of the Canticle of Creatures, St. Francis had received the Stigmata on LaVerna. We know from the accounts of Brother Celano, he suffered great physical and mental anguish. In a trance he heard a voice in his spirit advising him that his tribulations and illnesses were gifts of God's kingdom, a destination of which he is assured. In that moment he had a realization of a completely reconciled universe and overcomes all contradiction. He begins to sing *Altissimu, omnipotente, bon Signore*... God is the author of all that exists, and the natural elements have a symbolic worth. Leonardo Boff writes that humanity expresses by means of these elements an interior world...

> It expresses the emergence of a universal reconciliation, the fusion between cosmic mysticism, orientated toward fraternity with nature, and evangelical mysticism, orientated toward love for the person of Christ. The elements praised in the canticle gain an archetypal sacramentality, communicating this fusion[343].

The Canticle begins with an expression of deep humility before the creator and St. Francis' humility is reminiscent of the reverence the ancient Israelites had for the name of Yahweh. A shift takes place from focusing on the horizontal relationship with God to the vertical relationship with creation. Creatures become sacraments and the source of encounter with the Most High. The language used by St. Francis is like Genesis and the Psalms where creation is portrayed as

---

[342] Joshtrom Isaac Kureethadam, *The Ten Green Commandments of Laudato Si*, Minnesota, Liturgical Press, 1994, p. 126.

[343] Lenoardo Boff, *Francis of Assisi*, New York, Orbis Books, 1982, p.38.

intrinsically good because of its divine origin. The totality of the human person is expressed through masculine and feminine pairings, beginning with Sir Brother Sun, and ending with Sister Mother Earth. The themes running through the Canticle are at the level of ontogeny, utility, beauty, fraternity, symbolism, and sacrament[344]. For example, St. Francis connects water with baptism and penance when referring to it as humble, useful, precious, and pure. By referring to the elements in familial terms he relates to them as he would a member of his family. The totality of the human person is expressed through masculine and feminine pairings beginning with Sir Brother Sun and ending with Sister Mother Earth.

The Canticle is full of emotion and a childlike innocence. It is evident St. Francis is highly sensitized to complex relationship between humanity and creation and their mutual dependence on God. He maintains the hierarchical character of creation consistent with the medieval tradition. Throughout he references usefulness and productiveness. The Canticle is written to stimulate gratitude for creation within the reader. The reverence for God in the beginning is followed with enjoyment and delight at contemplation of the natural environment. The bridge phrase "Be Praised" expresses St. Francis' joy at God's creation. St. Francis develops the normal medieval approach to the natural world characterised by its Biblical, symbolic, and sacramental approach and adds yet another dimension, en-fraternization. Roger D. Sorrell writes…

> Francis similarly envisioned a harmonious and interdependent community of creation. His concern for creatures and his desire that people respect and appreciate them demonstrate this conception of autonomy and reciprocity. His use of familial and chivalric address to creatures was not pantheistic, romantic, or oppressive (in a sexist manner). Rather it was a step toward balancing a perceived "I-it" objectifying relationship and an "I-thou"

---

[344] Roger D. Sorrell, *St. Francis of Assisi, and Nature: Tradition and innovation in Western Christian Attitudes toward the Environment,* Oxford, Oxford University Press, 1988, p.125.

relationship of respect and affection between humans and creatures[345].

St. Francis' attitude toward creation is one of submission, respect, and mutual service. Each creature has a separate autonomy, integrity, and usefulness. He advocates reconciliation between humanity and the natural environment and acceptance of our own mortality[346]. This will create and restore, not paradise lost, but harmony between creatures, humanity, and God. St. Francis is the patron of ecology because he understands the proper place of humanity in the community of creation.

---

[345] Roger D. Sorrell, *St. Francis of Assisi, and Nature: Tradition and innovation in Western Christian Attitudes toward the Environment,* Oxford, Oxford University Press, 1988, p.134.

[346] Regis J. Armstrong. O.F.M. Cap.(ed.), J. A. Wayne Hellman, O.F.M. Conv.(ed.), William J. Short, O.F.M., (ed.), St. Francis of Assisi the Saint: Early Documents, New York, New City Press, 1999, p. 144.

Ecumenical Initiatives

Ecumenical dialogue and exchange foster a deeper understanding of the theology of creation[347]. One positive aspect of the ecological crisis is the potential for ecumenical collegiality to ensure ecological stewardship. The culture of domination which spread and developed throughout Europe and North America is closely related to the process of colonisation. Part of the process of ecological conversion and developing an ecological spirituality will be learning from the mistakes of the past. Inter-Church dialogue will be essential to form a theology of creation, after all, the crisis affects everyone regardless of their creed. The Catholic vision of 'receive and pass on' may of course be applied to the environment however we must remember this will not be possible without international collaboration.

One Church from which we may learn about developing an ecological spirituality is the Greek Orthodox Church. In *Laudato Si'* Pope Francis highlights the contributions to the environmental debate made by Ecumenical Patriarch Bartholomew. The contribution of the Greek Orthodox Church deserves further attention to understand the depth and uniqueness of their environmental initiatives. Their efforts date back to 1987 and include prayer services for creation, issuance of statements, and environmental seminars. The desire for the union of the Roman Catholic Church and the Greek Orthodox Church is stronger now than ever and perhaps a shared theology of creation will be a way to advance this cause.

Our starting point is the World Day of Prayer for Creation in 1989. At this time, the Patriarch Dimitrios declared the Orthodox

---

[347] Kevin W. Irwin, *A Commentary on Laudato Si': Examining the Background, Contributions, Implementation, and Future of Pope Francis's Encyclical*, New York, Paulist Press, 2016, p. 24.

Churches would celebrate the World Day of Prayer for the protection of the environment on September the first, the first day of their liturgical year. The liturgy on this day included prayers of praise, thanksgiving, and intercession for creation. Each year on the first of September the Patriarch issues a statement. These letters outline the ecological vision of the Orthodox Church. The Patriarch Dimitrios evidently supports a collective response to levels of consumption and advocates an 'ascetic ethos' towards the use of the Earth's resources stating we are called to be stewards not proprietors. Pope Francis made the decision in 2015 to join the Orthodox in celebrating the World Day of Prayer on the same date and have ecumenical representatives at the service[348].

On October 22nd, 1991, the Patriarch Bartholomew was elected archbishop of Constantinople and Ecumenical Patriarch due to the death of Dimitrios. He continued the tradition of issuing a letter on the World Day of Prayer for Creation. He often emphasised the centrality of the human person between the material and spiritual creation and how this increases our responsibility for the created world. He understands our responsibility to be responsible stewards of the gift of creation as a collective responsibility. The Patriarch advocates the celebration of the Eucharist as one alternative in order to be partakers in worship and not consumers. For whenever we place a sacramental lens on creation, we begin to include a theology of the Eucharist and the liturgy in our ecological ethos. The Patriarch states what is needed is an environmental ethic that is Eucharistic accompanied by doxology toward God. As we are baptised priest, prophet, and king in the eternal kingdom we should exhibit a similar attitude towards the environment here and now.

Patriarch Bartholomew assures his readers the environmental crisis is, at its root, a spiritual crisis. Because of this reconciliation and prayer is necessary to re-establish a true and stable relationship between humanity and the rest of creation as our relationship with the environment will develop in parallel to our relationship with God. The logic of arrogance needs to be replaced with ecological

---

[348] Kevin W. Irwin, *A Commentary on Laudato Si': Examining the Background, Contributions, Implementation, and Future of Pope Francis's Encyclical*, New York, Paulist Press, 2016, p. 60 – 61.

conversion to respect the integrity of every living creature. Humanity has made the mistake of loving creation more than the creator, making an idol out of creation. In 2012 Patriarch Bartholomew acknowledged that the source of abuses to the environment is humans themselves and the destruction is observable by scientists and religious leaders alike. There is a strong ethical tone in the Greek Orthodox attitude toward scientific research. Any activities invisible to the naked eye that may potentially bring imbalance and destruction to the environment e.g., changes to genetics and the catastrophic potential of atomic manipulation, are to be utterly condemned. This is not to condemn scientific research however we need to discern if advancements are ethical or not. The Orthodox Church constantly strives to help humanity focus on the ethical and theological consequences of their actions.

The teachings and writings of Patriarch Bartholomew are quoted a number of times in *Laudato Si'*. First his emphasis on the need to repent for ecological damage and the ways we have harmed the planet is quoted (*LS* 8)[349]. He states each of us are called to acknowledge our contribution to the destruction of creation. Our sinfulness is the result of destroying biological diversity, degrading the integrity of the earth causing changes to the climate, stripping the earth of natural forests and wetlands, and contaminating the Earth's water, land, and air. A sin against the natural world is tantamount to a sin against our-selves and God. The root of this sin is in the refusal to view life and the world as a sacrament of thanksgiving and as a gift of constant communication with God on a global scale[350]. Patriarch Bartholomew teaches the monastic way of life, expressed as a new asceticism, can be an ecological corrective. He sees the solutions to the environmental crisis as being not only in technology but also in a change of mindset and attitude. The Greek Orthodox

---

[349] Pope Francis, *Laudato Si': On Care for Our Common Home*, London, Catholic Truth Society, 2015, p. 10.

[350] Patriarch Bartholomew, *Address of Ecumenical Patriarch Bartholomew at the Environmental Symposium, Saint Barbara Greek Orthodox Church*, [website], 1997, Address of Ecumenical Patriarch Bartholomew at the Environmental Symposium, Saint Barbara Greek Orthodox Church, Santa Barbara, California - The Environment - Apostolic Pilgrimage of Pope Francis and Ecumenical Patriarch Bartholomew to Jerusalem, (accessed 27th February 2021).

Church advocates monasticism and the ascetic way of life as a way to restore ecological balance as monks and nuns represent the spirit of asceticism and self-restraint. Patriarch Bartholomew refers to the Cross as a single solution to the ecological crisis as it reminds us of the reality of human failure and the need for cosmic repentance. The Cross inspires us to a radical reversal of our perspectives and practices and proposes a solution of self-denial. A spirit of asceticism will lead us to a spirit of gratitude and love as we rediscover the wonder and beauty of the universe. Asceticism helps to develop self-control (*enkrateia*) which will ensure the limitation of food consumption and natural resources. He encourages the practice of fasting for affirming the sacredness of material creation, and for healing and restoration. This is an acknowledgement that material creation is not under our control to be exploited selfishly but should be returned in thanks and restored in an act of communion with God[351]. Fasting leads us to share and connect with others. It helps us to be liberated from fear, greed and compulsion and allows us to begin to love. When we love the gift of creation a shift in attitude takes place from focusing on what I want to what God's world needs[352]. Patriarch Bartholomew is profound when he states that we will address ecological issues on our knees and not only in the public sphere and political domain. Bartholomew reiterates the theme of the world as a sacrament of communion with God in his closing remarks at the Halki Summit on 20th June 2012. The divine and the human meet in the seamless garment of God's creation, and even in the last speck of dust on our planet.

There have been numerous joint statements on the environment between the Catholic Church and the Greek Orthodox Church. In 2002 Pope John Paul II and Patriarch Bartholomew issued a joint statement at the Fourth Ecological Symposium on the Adriatic Sea. Both Church leaders call for repentance and highlight the need to contextualise the universe within the divine design. Both agree the climate crisis is fundamentally a moral and spiritual crisis and not an

---

[351] Patriarch Bartholomew, *The Ascetic Corrective: Lecture at the Monastery of Utstein*, [website], 2003, The Ascetic Corrective (Patriarch Bartholomew of Constantinople) | MYSTA GOGY RESOURCE CENTER (johnsanidopoulos.com), (accessed 27th February 2021).

[352] Ibid.

economic and technological crisis and therefore a solution will demand a change in heart and lifestyle and not necessarily a reorientation towards economics and technology. The Orthodox church teaching lays the foundation for the teaching of Pope Francis in *Laudato Si'* in stating that changing the way we think, and act can only be accomplished through a genuine conversion to Christ. This inner conversion is necessary first before we will change our modern lifestyles characterised with unsustainable patterns of consumption and production.

Pope John Paul II and Patriarch Bartholomew II outlined seven factors for a new approach in thought action and prayer. First our actions need to consider future generations, i.e., the Children who will be affected by the decisions we make. Secondly our decisions need to take into consideration the natural laws sustaining humanity. Thirdly science and technology should be involved in a possible solution to the climate crisis insofar as it is anthropocentric, focused on the common good, and preserves the integrity of creation. Fourthly, ownership needs to be considered in terms of the social mortgage, and always display solidarity with those who are less well off. Therefore, we should not take irreversible actions in this life with what we regard as our property. Fifth, there is a diversity of responsibilities related to achieving climate justice. Every person, institution and country does not have the same burden to bear. Those countries which inflict the most damage to the environment have the greater responsibility in absorbing costs related to reversing the damage. The responsibilities of religions, governments and institutions are best founded on the principal of subsidiarity thus ensuring affluent societies carry a heavier burden than the poor. The sixth point is to peacefully embrace dialogue about how to best live on the earth, share and use its resources, and what to change and leave unchanged. Controversy should not be evaded as humanity can reason and reach agreement. Solutions to disagreement will only be achieved through open exchange. Finally, the seventh point of the joint statement between the Roman Catholic and Greek Orthodox

Church is that it is not too late for the earth to replenish its eco-system and guarantee a better future for the next generation[353].

On 25th May 2014, Pope Francis and Bartholomew issued a joint declaration in Jerusalem on the depth and authenticity of their existing bonds. In this statement they highlight how the future of the human family will depend on how we safeguard the gift entrusted to us by the creator. This gift needs to be safeguarded prudently and compassionately with justice and fairness. Both leaders acknowledge in repentance the wrongful mistreatment of our planet which is tantamount to a sin in the eyes of God[354]. Both reaffirmed our responsibility and obligation to foster humility and moderation so all may sense the need to respect creation and feel a personal responsibility to safeguard it with care. Both leaders reassert their commitment to raising awareness about the responsible stewardship of creation and encourage less wasteful and frugal lifestyles which are more generous than greedy. This joint statement contains many of the themes contained in *Laudato Si'* which is published a year later in 2015. In a joint statement of ten paragraphs, it is significant that one paragraph is dedicated to the state of the planet. It is indicative of the importance of climate justice for both the Orthodox and Roman Catholic Church.

The theology of creation offers different faiths the opportunity to enter ecumenical dialogue. The joint statements from the Roman Catholic and Greek Orthodox church is evidence of how dialogue can lead to mutual enrichment. The Western and Eastern traditions both have different approaches to creation as in the west the point of departure is creation, and the point of arrival is Christ and the revelation of the Trinity. Whereas the East begins with the mystery of the Trinity and arrives at the unfolding of the economy of creation and salvation[355]. The spirituality in the Orthodox Church, developed

---

[353] Kevin W. Irwin, *A Commentary on Laudato Si': Examining the Background, Contributions, Implementation, and Future of Pope Francis's Encyclical*, New York, Paulist Press, 2016, p. 70-71.

[354] Pope Francis and Patriarch Bartholomew, *Joint Declaration by Pope Francis, and Patriarch Bartholomew*, [website], 2014, Joint Declaration - Apostolic Pilgrimage of Pope Francis and Ecumenical Patriarch Bartholomew to Jerusalem, (accessed 28th January 2021).

[355] Paul Haffner, *Mystery of Creation*, Herefordshire, Gracewing, 1995, p. 24.

from the Christian vision of creation, is important for the moral education of its members. Although the emphasis on the East is on cosmology and freedom rather than morality and obedience. All of creation finds its purpose and perfection in the liturgy alone. For the Orthodox faith humanity is called to a priestly vocation i.e., to praise and honour God and to cleanse and heal creation. In the East, the language of gift and blessing is preferred to the language of stewardship and dominion[356]. In the East, the Church is co-extensive with the *cosmos* and also in need of redemption (Is 11: 6-9).

The Greek Orthodox Church is not the only church the Roman Catholic Church has issued a joint statement with on the environment. Participants in the Roman Catholic-United Methodists dialogue on the Eucharist and Ecology issued joint statements from 2008 – 2012. The purpose was to glean and discern a common stance on the Eucharist and Ecology[357]. Both Churches sought to join the company of heaven in praising God in creation and identify the celebration of the Eucharist as a thanksgiving for the gifts of creation. Ecology and the climate crisis is not a disputed doctrine between Catholicism and Methodism, it is a common concern. Both churches express a desire to work together to achieve justice for God's creation through obedience to the divine creator and give gratitude for the gift of creation through the celebration of the Eucharist. The relationship between humanity and the natural world, which is disordered, is a challenge for both communions. Both the Roman Catholic Church and the Methodist church interpret climate destabilization, destruction of the ozone and the loss of biodiversity, as signs of the times which necessitate an ecumenical response. The joint statement highlights the significance of the work of human hands in the presentation of the gifts during the liturgy and sees the presence of the divine in humanity and nature.

Declarations on the climate emergency are not restricted to Christianity. For example, in 2015 an Islamic declaration on climate was released at Istanbul. This indicates the support for climate action

---

[356] Paul Haffner, *Mystery of Creation*, Herefordshire, Gracewing, 1995, p. 304.

[357] Kevin W. Irwin, *A Commentary on Laudato Si': Examining the Background, Contributions, Implementation, and Future of Pope Francis's Encyclical*, New York, Paulist Press, 2016, p. 72.

within the world's largest denomination. The release of the statement coincided with the launch of the Global Muslim Climate Network and the signing of the Paris Climate Agreement. The statement was endorsed by over eight Muslim leaders. The statement asks for nations with greater responsibility and capacity to lead the way in fossil fuel diversification and shift to completely renewable energy resources. The statement reinforces the Islamic teaching that man is a steward of the earth's resources and, calls for nations to reduce their green-house gas emissions. The statement also calls for support for vulnerable communities. The Global Muslim Climate Network will ensure engagement in climate action at local, national, and international levels. One such initiative includes the 'Green Ramadan' project to encourage Muslim governments to diversify from fossil fuels to renewable energies[358].

In the same year in 2015, 425 rabbis signed a rabbinic letter on the climate crisis. The statement called for immediate and vigorous action to prevent the climate crisis from worsening and highlighted the need to seek social justice. The statement begins acknowledging the importance of science for explaining the way in which the universe works. They restate their belief in the divine gift of creation and the presence of the divine hand in every creature. For the rabbis, part of the solution to the climate crisis is a joyful human voice and a healing human hand. They find the origins modern science's findings in the *Torah's* insights about the need to heal the relationship between humanity and the Earth. They reference the teaching in Leviticus 25-26 and Deuteronomy 15 where one year in every seven should be a sabbatical year. This provides a year of rest for the labourers and the earth[359]. This leads them to state the crisis in our planet finds its origins in not paying attention to a warning from the ancient indigenous people in Israel regarding the over working of the earth. The rabbis understand the current crisis as the embodiment of Leviticus 26 and finds a possible solution in the ancient wisdom of

---

[358] Muslim Leaders, *Muslim Leaders Deliver Islamic Climate Change Declarations*, [website], 2015, Muslim leaders deliver Islamic climate change declaration | Islamic Relief Worldwide (islamic-relief.org), (accessed 1st March 2021).

[359] Rabbi Arthur Waskow, *A Rabbinic Letter on the Climate Crisis*, [website], 2015, Rabbinic Letter on Climate -Torah, Pope, & Crisis Inspire 425+ Rabbis to Call for Vigorous Climate Action | The Shalom Center, (accessed 1st March 2021).

the Sh'ma. They speak of the unity of all things and the interwovenness of all creatures including the divine. Lessons from the past have taught us that if we continue with current consumption, we will create refugees. The rabbis call for a new sense of what they refer to as 'eco-social justice'[360] which the Torah makes possible. For Biblical Israel this is a central question in their relationship with Yahweh. The challenge today is to turn inherited wisdom into action and redirect investment from the 'modern pharaoh's' to initiatives that will help to heal the earth. They write… "Our ancient earthly wisdom taught that social justice, sustainable abundance, a healthy Earth, and spiritual fulfilment are inseparable. Today we must hear that teaching in a world-wide context, drawing upon our unaccustomed ability to help shape public policy in a great nation. We call upon Jewish people to meet God's challenge once again"[361].

---

[360] Rabbi Arthur Waskow, *A Rabbinic Letter on the Climate Crisis*, [website], 2015, Rabbinic Letter on Climate -Torah, Pope, & Crisis Inspire 425+ Rabbis to Call for Vigorous Climate Action | The Shalom Center, (accessed 1st March 2021).

[361] Ibid.

Conclusion

Climate change is not a scientific abstraction but a man-made phenomenon impacting people, particularly the most vulnerable, all over the world[362]. This man-made phenomenon is inextricably linked with injustice leading to poverty, exclusion, and inequality. The existing technocratic paradigm leading to a culture of compulsive consumerism is at odds with Biblical models of creation. The evidence for the urgent need to change our current lifestyles is overwhelming as we strive to find and re-establish humanities proper place within the *cosmos.* An essential element in the journey toward climate justice will be the realization of the interdependence and interconnectedness of humanity and creation[363] . This realization will lead us to caring responsibility for all creatures, the Earth, and to understand creation as a divine gift for which we are responsible. We find our rightful place within the community model of creation through integral ecology and dialogue with other disciplines.

The present climate emergency is but a symptom of a deep-rooted moral crisis within humanity. The root of the moral crisis is in modern man's utilitarian world view leading to a throw-a-way culture, and lack of humility. This moral crisis within humanity may only be resolved when we understand ecological degradation as being sinful due to the damage we do to the environment, the disproportionate effects of the crisis on the poor, and the kind of world we are leaving for future generations. Climate justice may only be achieved through an ecological conversion inspiring us to solidarity with all inhabitants in our common home. Repentance and

---

[362] Mary Robinson, *Climate Justice: Hope, resilience and the Fight for Sustainable Future*, London, Bloomsbury, 2018, p. 3.

[363] Richard Bauckham, Bible and Ecology, London, Darton Longman and Todd, 2019, p. 33.

reconciliation between individuals, communities and nations will contribute to achieving climate justice.

The teaching of the Church, in relation to the *cosmos,* has gained impetus from Vatican II to the publication of *Laudato Si'* in 2015. The contributions to the debate from John Paul II are significant when compared with his predecessors as this is a modern crisis brought about and caused by modern man. The teaching from the pontiffs, particularly in the last fifty years, have contextualized the climate emergency within the corpus of the Catholic Social Teaching and provided a framework and guidelines for the necessary change in attitude and lifestyles.

The patron for ecologists is St. Francis of Assisi. The reason for this is St. Francis has an exemplary attitude and understanding of the place of humanity in the *cosmos.* His familial relationship with creation and humanity finds expression in the 'Canticle of Creatures' where he refers to the Sun as 'brother' and the Moon as his 'sister'. St. Francis' lived a life expressing the 'Kinship-Community' model of creation. This model finds its origins in the creation theology of the Hebrew Bible as expressed in Psalm 104 and in the extract from the Sermon on the Mount in Matthew 6: 25-33. Jesus turns the teaching of Psalm 104 into advice on how the disciples should have faith in God's ability to provide for his creatures. God's lovingkindness for his creatures liberates the disciples to prioritise seeking and building the Kingdom of God. St. Francis develops this radical teaching into a rule for the Franciscan Community. He is the patron of ecologists because he lived in total harmony with his community, creation and with God and his example offers a remedy for modern ills.

Just as there is an urgent need for a radical change in lifestyle, there is also a need for us to re-establish the connection with creation in our worship and liturgy. In fact, the liturgy provides a sacred space for ongoing ecological conversion. The celebration of the Eucharist is possible only with the gifts of creation indicating all of creation is orientated toward the worship of the divine master. The current crisis provides the opportunity for ongoing ecumenical dialogue and the publication of joint statements related to theology of the natural world.

Bibliography

AHLQUIST Dale, *The Complete Thinker: The Marvellous mind of G.K. Chesterton*, San Francisco: Ignatius Press, 2012

Ed., ARMSTRONG, Regis J. O.F.M., Cap., HELLMANN, Wayne J.A. O.F.M., Conv., SHORT William J. O.F.M., *Francis of Assisi: The Saint*, New York: New City Press, 1999

SAINT AUGUSTINE, *City of God*, London: Penguin Books, 2003

BAUCKHAM Richard, *Bible and Ecology: Rediscovering the Community of Creation*, London: Darton Longman and Todd, 2019

BENEDICT XVI, Pope, *The Garden of God: Toward a Human Ecology*, Washington, D.C.: The Catholic University of America Press, 2014

BOFF Leonardo, *Francis of Assisi*, New York: Orbis Books, 1982

BOFF Leonardo, *When Theology Listens to the Poor*, New York: Harper and Row, 1988

BOFF Leonardo, *Cry of the Earth, Cry of the Poor*, New York: Orbis Books, 1997

Ed., BROWN Raymond E., FITZMYER Joseph A., MURPHY, Roland E., *The New Jerome Biblical Commentary*, London: Geoffrey Chapman, 1993

CHADWICK Henry, *The Early Church: The Story of Emergent Christianity from the Past Apostolic Age to the Dividing of the Ways Between the Greek East and the Latin West*, New York: Penguin Books, 1990

C.S. LEWIS, *Reflections on the Psalms*, London: William Collins, 1958

CONGREGATION FOR THE DOCTRINE OF THE FAITH, *Lumen Gentium: On the Church Vatican Council II*, London: Catholic Truth Society, 2012

Ed., CROSS, F.L., LIVINGSTONE E.A., *The Oxford Dictionary of the Christian Church*, New York: Oxford University Press, 1983

Division of Christian Education of the National Council of the Churches of Christ in the United States of America, *The Holy Bible,* San Francisco: Ignatius Press, 2006

DORR, Donal, *Option for the Poor: A Hundred Years of Vatican Social Teaching,* Dublin: Gill and MacMillian, 1983

HAFFNER, Paul, *Mystery of Creation*, Herefordshire: Gracewing, 2010

IRWIN, Kevin, W., *A Commentary on Laudato Si': Examining the Background, Contributions, Implementations, and Future of Pope Francis's Encyclical,* New York: Paulist Press, 2016

Ed., HESSEL Dieter T., RUETHER Rosemary Radford, *Christianity, and Ecology: Seeking the Well Being of Earth and Humans,* Cambridge: Harvard University Press, 2000

KUREETHADAM, Joshtrom Isaac, *The Ten Green Commandments of Laudato Si',* Collegeville: Liturgical Press, 2019

LANE Dermott A., *Theology and Ecology in Dialogue: The Wisdom of Laudato Si',* Dublin: Messenger Publications, 2020

LORBIECKI, Marybeth, *Following St. Francis: John Paul II's Call for Ecological Action*, New York: Rizzoli ex libris, 2014

FRANCIS POPE, *Laudato Si': On Care for our Common Home,* London: Catholic Truth Society, 2015

FRANCIS POPE, *Querida Amazonia, The Amazon: new paths for the Church and for an Integral Ecology*, Hampshire: Redemptorist Publication, 2020

ROBINSON Mary, *Climate Justice: Hope Resilience and the Fight for a Sustainable Future*, London: Bloomsbury Publishing, 2018

RUSTON Roger, *Human Rights and the Image of God*, London: SCM Press, 2004

BIBLIOGRAPHY

SORRELL, Roger D., *St. Francis of Assisi, and Nature: Tradition and Innovation in Western Christian Attitudes Toward the Environment*, Oxford: Oxford University Press, 1988

THUNBERG Greta, *No One is Too Small to Make a Difference*, London: Penguin Books, 2019

Ed., VAN HOUTAN, Kyle S., NORTHCOTT, Michael S., *Diversity and Dominion: Dialogues in Ecology, Ethics and Theology*, Oregon: Cascade Books, 2010

INDEX

DOMUNI-PRESS
publishing house of DOMUNI University

« Le livre grandit avec le lecteur »
"The book grows with the reader."

The University

Domuni University was founded in 1999 by French Dominicans. It offers Bachelor, Master and Doctorate degrees by distance learning, as well as "à la carte" (stand-alone) courses and certificates in philosophy, theology, religious sciences, and social sciences (including both state and canonical diplomas). It welcomes several thousand students on its teaching platform, which operates in five languages: French, English, Spanish, Italian, and Arabic. The platform is accompanied by more than three hundred professors and tutors. Anchored in the Order of Preachers, Domuni University benefits from its centuries-old tradition of study and research. Innovative in many ways, Domuni consists of an international network that offers courses to students worldwide.

To find out more about Domuni:

www.domuni.eu

The publishing house

Domuni-Press disseminates research and publishes works in the academic fields of interest of Domuni University: theology, philosophy, spirituality, history, religions, law and social sciences. Domuni-Press is part of a lively research community located at the heart of the Dominican network. Domuni-Press aims to bring readers closer to their texts by making it possible, via the help of today's digital technology, to have immediate access to them, while ensuring a quality paperback edition. Each work is published in both forms. The key word is simplicity. The subjects are approached with a clear editorial line: academic quality, accessible to all, with the aim of spreading the richness of Christian thought. Six collections are available: theology, philosophy, spirituality, Bible, history, law and social sciences. Domuni-Press has its own online bookshop: www.domunipress.fr. Its books are also available on its main distance selling website: Amazon, Fnac.com, and in more than 900 bookshops and sales outlets around the world.

To find out more about the publishing house:

www.domunipress.fr

EXTRACT FROM THE CATALOGUE

Paul TAVARDON, ocso,
Trappistes en terre sainte. Des moines au cœur de la géopolitique. Latroun, 1890-1946 (T.1).

Paul TAVARDON, ocso,
Trappistes en terre sainte. Des moines au cœur de la géopolitique. Latroun, 1946-1991 (T.2).

Marie MONNET (sous la direction de),
La source théologique du droit.

Nilson Léal DE SA,
La vie fraternelle.

Apollinaire KIVYAMUNDA,
Maurice Zundel. La relation à Dieu.

Lara LOYE,
Fraternités.

Bernadette ESCAFFRE,
Vocations. Quand Dieu appelle.

Raphaël HAAS,
Pleine conscience. Bouddhisme et christianisme en dialogue.

Augustin WILIWOLI,
Axel Honneth. Lutter pour la reconnaissance.

Louis FROUART,
Pascal. Cœur, Corps, Esprit.

Emmanuel BOISSIEU,
Platon. Une manière de vivre.

Emmanuel BOISSIEU,
Kant. Une philosophie de la liberté.

Marie MONNET,
Dieu migrant.

Thérèse HEBBELINCK,
L'Église catholique et les juifs (T.1 et T.2).

Béatrice PAPASOGLOU,
Qu'est-ce que l'homme ?

Augustin WILIWOLI SIBILONI op,
   Ce que les philosophes disent du vivre-ensemble.

François MENAGER,
   Yves Bonnefoy, poète et philosophe.

Nicole AWAIS,
   L'art d'enseigner le fait religieux.

Thérèse M. ANDREVON,
   Une théologie à la frontière (T.1 et T2).

Michel VAN AERDE,
   Venez vous reposer. Antidotes spirituels au burn-out.

Agnès GODEFROY,
   Bien vieillir, dans les pas d'Abraham.

Olivier BELLEIL,
   Résolution des conflits dans l'Église primitive.

Anton MILH op & Stephan VAN ERP,
   Identité et visibilité. Conflits de générations chez les Dominicains.

Denis LABOURE,
   Astrologie et religion au Moyen Age.

Jorel FRANÇOIS,
   Voltaire, philosophe de la religion.

Augustin WILIWOLI SIBILONI op,
   La reconnaissance. Réparer les blessures.

Jean Baptiste ZEKE,
   Loi naturelle et post-humanisme.

Emmanuel BOISSIEU,
   Paul Ricœur. Un inconditionnel de l'amour.

Ameer JAJE,
   Le chiisme. Clés historiques et théologiques.

Jean-René PEGGARY,
   L'aube d'une pensée américaine. L'individu chez H. D. Thoreau.

Jean-François ARNOUX,
   Comme un feu dévorant. Flammèches d'une lecture incarnée de la Bible.

Olivier BELLEIL,
L'autre dans l'islam coranique.

Sœur Agnès DE LA CROIX,
Miroir juif des évangiles.

Jean-Michel COSSE,
Au centre de l'âme.

Jean-Paul BALDAZZA,
Antoine. Un saint d'Orient et d'Occident.

Ameer JAJE,
Marie dans l'islam.

Olivier PERRU,
Le corps malade.

Jesmond MICALLEF,
Trinitarian Ontology.

Abel TOE,
Pauvreté et développement au Burkina-Faso.

Jude Thaddeus MBI AKEM,
Le développement en Afrique.

Claude LICHTERT,
Lire la Bible ensemble.

Jorel FRANÇOIS,
Voltaire, philosophe contre le fanatisme.

Bruno CALLEBAUT,
Les Évangiles. Leurs origines, leurs exégèses.

Claude LICHTERT,
La parole pour sortir de soi. Dieu et les humains aujourd'hui : parcours biblique.

Heriberto CABRERA REYES,
Effondrement, apocalypse ou renaissance ? Théologie en temps de crise.

Patrick MONJOU,
Comment prêcher à la fin du Moyen Âge ? (T. 1 et T. 2).

Robert PLÉTY,
À la découverte du Rabbi de Nazareth (T. 1).

Robert PLÉTY,
À la rencontre du Rabbi de Nazareth (T. 2).

Jules KATSURANA,
Guide pour la Prévention de la violence sexiste.

Jacques FOURNIER,
La Trinité, mystère d'amour.

Louis D'HÉROUVILLE,
Marie-Madeleine, femme pascale.

Olivier PERRU,
Martin-Stanislas Gillet (1875-1951). La peur de l'effort intellectuel.

Paul-Marcel LEMAIRE,
Vivre l'Évangile.

John Jack LYNCH,
Judith, Sarah and Esther. Jewish heroines.

Paul NYAGA,
Moral Consistency with Lonergan's Thought.

François FAURE,
Emmanuel Mounier : La personne est son engagement (T. 1).

François FAURE,
Emmanuel Mounier : Montrer, sans démontrer (T. 2).

Olivier-Thomas VENARD, Gregory TATUM,
Conversations sur Paul. « Supportez-vous les uns les autres ».

Isaac MUTELO,
Muslim Organisations in South Africa. Political Role Post-1948.

Stephen Musisi KASOZI,
Issues of Constitutionalism. A case study of Uganda.

Pierre Dalin DOMERSON,
La gestion des biens de l'Église. Enjeu Pastoral.

Philippe ANDRÈS,
Notre-Dame de Rocamadour. Du Moyen Âge à nos jours.